Routledge Revivals

Education and Income Distribution in Asia

First published in 1981, *Education and Income Distribution in Asia* looks in detail at a number of aspects of the relation between education, employment, and income. Education is now the major programme of expenditure of governments in Asian countries. This book brings case studies from Philippines, India, Sri Lanka, and Thailand to discuss themes like equality in education; schooling, earnings, and occupation; educational expansion and the labour market; determinants of educational achievement; school enrolment in India, Sri Lanka, and Thailand; and educational innovations and inequality. This book is a must read for scholars and researchers of education, public policy, and economics.

Education and Income Distribution in Asia

A study prepared for the International Labour Office...

P. Richards and M. Leonor

First published in 1981
by Croom Helm

This edition first published in 2022 by Routledge
4 Park Square, Milton Park, Abingdon, Oxon, OX14 4RN

and by Routledge
605 Third Avenue, New York, NY 10017

Routledge is an imprint of the Taylor & Francis Group, an informa business

© 1981 International Labour Organization

All rights reserved. No part of this book may be reprinted or reproduced or utilised in any form or by any electronic, mechanical, or other means, now known or hereafter invented, including photocopying and recording, or in any information storage or retrieval system, without permission in writing from the publishers.

Publisher's Note
The publisher has gone to great lengths to ensure the quality of this reprint but points out that some imperfections in the original copies may be apparent.

Disclaimer
The publisher has made every effort to trace copyright holders and welcomes correspondence from those they have been unable to contact.

A Library of Congress record exists under ISBN: 0709922019

ISBN: 978-1-032-32189-9 (hbk)
ISBN: 978-1-003-31329-8 (ebk)
ISBN: 978-1-032-32191-2 (pbk)

Book DOI 10.4324/9781003313298

Education and Income Distribution in Asia

P. RICHARDS AND M. LEONOR

A study prepared for the International Labour Office
within the framework of the World Employment Programme

CROOM HELM LONDON

© 1981 International Labour Organisation
Croom Helm Ltd, 2-10 St John's Road, London SW11

British Library Cataloguing in Publication Data
Richards, P
    Education and income distribution in Asia.
    1. Income distribution – Asia
    2. Education – Asia
    I. Title   II. Leonor, M
    III. International Labour Office.
    World Employment Programme
    339.2'095   HC415.15
ISBN 0-7099-2201-9

The responsibility for opinions expressed in signed articles, studies and other contributions rests solely with their authors, and publication does not constitute an endorsement by the International Labour Office of the opinions expressed in them.

References to firm names and commercial products and processes do not imply the endorsement of the International Labour Office, and any failure to mention a particular firm, commercial product or process in connection with the technologies described in this volume is not a sign of disapproval.

The designations employed and the presentation of material do not imply the expression of any opinion whatsoever on the part of the International Labour Office concerning the legal status of any country or territory or of its authorities, or concerning the delimitation of its frontiers.

Printed in Great Britain by
Biddles Ltd, Guildford, Surrey

CONTENTS

Preface	
Introduction	9
1. Equality in Education	14
2. Schooling, Earnings and Occupation	25
3. Educational Expansion and the Labour Market	38
4. International Comparisons I (General Pattern of Inequality)	57
5. International Comparisons II (Thinking Ability of Children of Labourers and of Executives and Professionals)	62
6. Determinants of Educational Achievement in the Philippines	79
7. School Enrolment in India, Sri Lanka and Thailand	110
8. Educational Innovations and Inequality	148
9. Summary, Conclusions and Recommendations	173
Index	187

PREFACE

This is the fourth book in this series which was carried out under the ILO Income Distribution and Employment Programme. After *Industrialisation, Employment and Income Distribution: A Case Study of Hong Kong* by Ronald Hsia and Laurence Chau (1978), *Inflation, Income Distribution and X-Efficiency Theory* by Harvey Leibenstein (1980) and *Socio-economic Groups and Income Distribution in Mexico* by Wouter van Ginneken (1980), the present study is concerned with interaction between education and income distribution in Asia.

Education is now the major programme of expenditure of governments in Asian countries. Given the common picture of a youthful population and increasing rates of school enrolment, this sector must become even more important. In principle, education systems hold out the promise of equality of opportunity and of social mobility, which should combine to increase the chances of economic equality and improve income distribution. Furthermore, research has proved, again and again, that levels of schooling are positively related to levels of earned income. Expansion of education should, on these arguments, sooner or later lead to a more equal society.

This study by Peter Richards and Mauricio Leonor, both staff members of the International Labour Office, is less sanguine about the prospects of educational expansion in Asia leading to an improved distribution of income. Their study looks in detail at a number of aspects of the relation between employment and incomes; at the way that well-paid jobs are allocated within the labour market, at the problems of access to schooling for the children of the Asian poor and at the process of ability creation that takes place within schools. The novelty of this study lies in its integration of this process of ability creation with its analysis of the operation of labour markets and of access to schooling. Schools, the study concludes, set out to develop the attitudes most favourably rewarded by the labour market, whatever the shape or form of the school curriculum. But these abilities are precisely those for which development is most aided by the characteristics of already educated and slightly wealthier households. Furthermore, the study warns, the wrong type of educational expansion can lead to home background becoming even more decisive in the development of abilities. Thus, a fast rate of expansion of low-quality education could worsen the distribution of income.

Geneva, July 1980   Felix Paukert
                                Chief of the Income Distribution and
                          International Employment Policies Branch,
                                          International Labour Office

INTRODUCTION

> The human capital approach ... argues that concentration patterns in human skills are as important a cause of income inequality as the concentration of physical assets. *On this view public policy should aim as far as possible to promote education so as to develop a more equal pattern of distribution of human capital.*[1]

Even the first reported statement in the above quotation is questionable, but the second statement and implied policy recommendation can be downright dangerous. The promotion of education, which usually means simply its expansion, may equally well lead to the opposite of the effect intended, i.e. greater inequality in incomes and overall well-being. This observation is not just a facile witticism. Boudon, for instance, finds that in Western societies, 'educational growth as such has the effect of increasing rather than decreasing social and economic inequality, even in the case of an educational system that becomes more egalitarian'.[2] Consistent with this assertion, Thurow has shown that in the United States, a country which is a prominent example of educational expansion, schooling has only a negligible effect in reducing income inequality.[3] There may therefore be good reason to doubt whether Asian educational systems, despite a very fast rate of expansion in recent years, have become more egalitarian. This assertion may seem astonishing. Briefly, our argument would be that educational expansion may well spread resources more thinly and thus give greater weight to home background factors in determining the distribution of abilities created, even with a higher average number of years of education completed by the school-going population. We hope this argument will become clear from the text.

Just as one may doubt the conventional wisdom which sees in educational expansion a key to income redistribution, so one can also question such beliefs as that 'education — of the right type — increases the quality of labour input, leading to ... higher wage earnings' or that 'a shift from the "academic" towards greater emphasis on vocational training'[4] is a thrust in the right direction. We hope to show later that this notion of the right (or wrong) type of education is illusory (or at best largely undefined), even if *vocational training* is widely advocated as a solution for poverty by educators and by institutions which have persuasive influence on educational policy in poor countries. Further, we hope to show, too, that in the context of income distribution vocational training merely promises hope for the poor while keeping them from the education of the rich.

One major aim of this study is to stress that the link between education and income distribution can be seen in terms of two stages. Both involve clear associations of two variables, income on the one side, and educational achievement on the other, but refer to different time phases. In the first phase the household income of the parents is connected with the education of the children. If this connection is significant, then the distribution of parental income may be seen to affect the corresponding distribution of children's education, especially in terms of scholastic achievement.

In the next phase, i.e. when today's children become adults and move from school to the labour market, education acquired earlier influences the magnitude of the income they earn largely by determining their access to occupations; as in the first phase, the level and kind of education are likely to be linked to the size and distribution of incomes. Thus in the second phase the relationship is reversed and the stage is set for a repeat of the first phase along a long-term trajectory from one generation to another. Of course, there is no telling at any one moment whether this trajectory is upward, downward or level. Indeed, the whole crux of public educational policy is to find out how stable this trajectory is. Our preliminary impression is that it does tend to be stable.

In the first phase, the income of parents is associated with the intellectual achievement of children. The precise extent of this effect on ability will be investigated, using international data. In the second phase there is considerable evidence that additional education is associated with additional income. Such a finding is a basic datum, but it does not constitute even *prima facie* evidence that education can bring about an equalisation of incomes. In this study we shall explore the first phase in depth without neglecting the second. Wherever possible our approach will depart from the orthodox measurement of education in terms of years of schooling and will use scholastic achievement as measured by test scores as an indicator of education. For our discussion of the second phase such indicators are unfortunately not available and we shall therefore need to fall back at that stage on indicators based largely on years of schooling.

Our thesis is that educational achievement determines occupation; hence our concentration in this volume on schooling and children's

Introduction

education. The close relationships between levels of education and occupations of a particularly high level can be demonstrated. But we wish to stress one point, which we bring out strongly in Chapters 4 to 6, namely that 'achievements', by which in this context we mean abilities created, are the results of schooling, but that the same schooling does not guarantee results in every case, as we shall see in the next chapter. School systems themselves play a certain part here in the extent to which they allow, or enforce, repetition and thus screen for ability annually; where they do not do so the range of abilities associated with any particular class or grade will be greater. By stressing the importance of achievements, we demonstrate the increased importance of home background factors in schooling. Where attendance is the only criterion considered, the economic capacity of the family to support its offspring is accepted as the predominant influence. Once ability is added as another criterion, then parental education and exposure to books and other media at home, for example, must be brought into the formula. Naturally this will generally only increase further the importance of family income as a determinant of output.

We further believe that occupational structure is the main determinant of the distribution of work incomes. Our discussion, in Chapter 3, of the relative importance in the chain of causation determining income distribution, of education *per se* and of occupation, may not be conclusive. However, in many Asian countries the major role of public sector employment, where effective performance in a job may bring promotion to another slot but not a higher income in the current position, would support the belief stated at the beginning of this paragraph. Correspondingly, in self-employed agriculture, while education may very well improve the management of resources, it will not guarantee access to those resources; again occupation would predominate over education. But these considerations by no means make the distribution of education unimportant: it still plays a major part in determining future occupation and income.

The current distribution of schooling and of abilities developed would seem to be highly unequal. Whereas we show that years of education became slightly less unequally distributed in two countries, we certainly cannot show that abilities became more equally spread. In this respect schooling buttresses the distribution of occupations and can be used to 'justify' large differences in work incomes. As we make clear in the next chapter, we cannot expect, and would not expect, absolute equality in the distribution of abilities; we can only hope for a more equal spread. This will not come about, as we discuss in the final two chapters, if home background factors can play an equal or even an increasing role in the development of abilities: in that event the result will be the perpetuation of current inequalities. Nor will it come about if misguided attempts are made to shape school curricula to the child's expected future economic role: such attempts only impose a future economic role on whole communities and deny their younger members the opportunity of occupational change. Nor can the future roles of communities ever be safely predicted, and we therefore stress that curricula must be used to develop children's later ability to react and adjust to changing conditions.

In order not to overburden this study and to avoid a digression from our main theme, we do not discuss the relation of education to job-seeking, particularly of women and girls. We discuss, in Chapter 3, the depressing effects of open unemployment upon expected earnings by education category, but the data do not allow us to separate out these effects according to male and female job-seekers. However, it is possible that an increased desire of young women to take certain jobs has increased the labour supply and affected certain occupation-income links.

Another subject we did not broach was the possible effects of a diversion of government funds away from education towards other forms of investment. To discuss such an issue would involve the consideration of a very large number of imponderable factors, such as the productivity of different possible patterns of expenditure and the likelihood that better investment decisions would be taken; we feel that such a discussion can be fruitful only in a very specific national context.[5]

In this study we cover a broad range of issues concerning education, the labour market and income distribution. As will be seen, we came to feel that many of the links joining these issues together were strongly established and unlikely to change. In our concluding chapter we pick out particularly the 'multiple deprivation' of the poor (the interplay of low levels of physical resources and of knowledge, information, communications and influence), and set it alongside the hierarchical ranking which we find in terms of abilities and earnings. The result is depressing and, we feel, beyond the capacity of educational systems alone to change. Abilities are related to earnings in all societies, and 'multiple deprivation' makes it more difficult for the poor to develop abilities. Our conclusions and recommendations, however, are related not to the direction of overall change in society but to the support of such changes as may be expected from the educational system.

Introduction

While the division into the two time phases discussed above may be conceptually neat, it has not always been possible to separate the two phases completely in this study. Thus, Chapter 1 discusses notions of equality in education. These notions relate largely to the frontier between schooling and work, and to the measurement of the 'education' embodied in a school leaver. Chapter 2, however, concentrates on the second phase, and discusses some broad issues on the relation of education to employment and earnings. Chapter 3 concentrates on two countries, the Philippines and Sri Lanka, and asks to what use education generated by school systems has been put in the labour market. Both Chapters 2 and 3 point out the rewards to successful completion of an extended course of schooling; this observation is an essential element in understanding the role of education in the social system. Chapters 4 and 5 discuss international comparisons of academic ability using comparable test scores related to household background variables of the children tested. They therefore bring the discussion back to a concentration on the first phase. Chapters 6 and 7 discuss academic ability and enrolment and promotion at school in relation to household background variables, using national sources of information from India, the Philippines, Sri Lanka and Thailand. They serve to point out many of the social factors associated with education. Chapter 8 then reviews the changes in their educational systems which countries are currently undertaking, especially in the content of education and the likelihood that these changes will have beneficial consequences for income equality. Chapter 9 summarises the results of the study.

Notes

1. Montek S. Ahluwalia, 'The Scope for Policy Intervention' in Hollis Chenery et al., *Redistribution with Growth* (Oxford, Oxford University Press, 1974), p. 81 (our emphasis).
2. Raymond Boudon, *Education, Opportunity and Social Inequality: Changing Prospects on Western Society* (New York, John Wiley and Sons, 1974), p. 187.
3. Lester Thurow, 'Education and Economic Equality', *Public Interest*, No. 28, Summer 1972. See also the contrary views of Jacob Mincer, 'Progress in Human Capital Analyses of the Distribution of Earnings' in A.B. Atkinson (ed.), *The Personal Distribution of Incomes* (London, George Allen and Unwin, 1976); and of Barry Chiswick, *Income Inequalities* (New York, National Bureau of Economic Research, 1974).
4. Ahluwalia, 'Policy Intervention', p. 82.
5. Furthermore, our focus in this study is on education as a programme with its own objectives. These are the objectives of 'learning to learn', so that all individuals can decide on the wider purposes of their lives.

1 EQUALITY IN EDUCATION

A declaration of principles such as 'equal educational opportunity for everyone' raises people's hopes but it is virtually empty rhetoric unless the criteria on which judgements are made are specified. Anderson and Bowman[1] cite the following variants of that principle and bring into sharp focus the emptiness of such a phrase and the complexity of the problem:

(a) *An equal amount of education for everyone.* 'Amount' is vague, and could be measured in different ways. Equality in one measure of education does not necessarily imply equality in another. The same number of years spent in schooling do not necessarily lead to equality in the amounts or kinds of skills and knowledge learned. Equalisation of this kind can lead to qualitative differentiation.
(b) *Sufficient education to bring everyone to a given standard.* This is the notion of minimum needs in education. A 'poverty line' is fixed and everyone must be brought to a point above that line. An example of this approach is 'universal primary education'; the criterion of measurement is usually completion of a certain number of years of schooling. As pointed out above, that is a somewhat dubious measure of equality.
(c) *Sufficient education for everyone to reach his/her potential.* Human potential is largely undefined and its limits are virtually unknown. Only a very wealthy country could afford to bring individuals even to a very crude approximation of their potentials. In any event, if potential varies from one individual to another, the development of that potential need not spell equality in any other sense.[2]
(d) *Continued education provided gains in learning per input of teaching match an agreed norm.* This is, in fact, an approximation to the previous principle with the addition of a constraint, i.e. an agreed norm.

Among educators, equality of educational opportunity is seen in such diverse terms as 'a common curriculum for all children regardless of background', 'diversified curricula to meet the various needs of different types of students' or 'a common school system that is open to all children without any distinction'.[3] However, a common curriculum does not in any way lead to equality of educational results. The same curriculum followed in different environments (e.g. rural and urban) does not yield the same level of achievement. Neither would a common school system. Hence, these notions are quite remote from what might bring about any semblance of measured equality.

If we cannot specify the meaning of 'equality', will it help to investigate the notion of inequality? 'Inequality' suggests that a standard or norm exists which can be used as a reference point to determine deviations from that norm. Without such a norm, inequality is subject to many interpretations and ambiguities. For example, in a country of several ethnic groups, which educational attainment is to be used as a norm? That of the dominant ethnic group? The country's average level of schooling attained? That of the cultural minorities? This may seem to be a simple issue, but it is a delicate one.

For countries which subscribe to the Universal Declaration of Human Rights, it would seem that appeals to absolute equality pose no serious problem. The scholastic achievement of dominant groups may well be used as a convenient and acceptable reference point for focusing attention on groups which perform below that level. It must be recognised, however, that a single-minded pursuit of parity in educational achievement is fine until questions of efficiency arise. Then within constraints of efficiency, it will be necessary to specify various levels of inequality and the pace at which they are to be reduced.

Definitions and Measurements

Clearly there are some problems. Can we not specify some of the dimensions of educational inequality and mark off some reference points? From these benchmarks, a relative concept of equality may be formed with a reasonable degree of precision and accuracy. Let us consider some examples of reference points.

We can first of all ask what it is that we are trying to equalise in the education field. Education (or, in this context, more specifically, schooling) can be viewed as a production process in itself. It has inputs, processes and outcomes. In simple terms, inputs consist of all resources that are combined to bring about a teaching-learning process. Schools and their facilities, programmes, teachers and their qualifications and teaching time are examples of educational inputs. So too are pupils, and their learning time as well as their learning capacity may be regarded as examples of those inputs. The educational process is the teaching-learning process, and its immediate outcomes are knowledge, skills and attitudes. By lumping together the process with the inputs, attention can be focused on two entities, namely inputs and results. Should educational policy seek to equalise either of these, and if so which? Equalising inputs does not equalise results; and if equality of results is the objective, the inputs would probably need to be unequal.

The next question concerns the units among which inequality is to be assessed. At the lowest level, the individual is such a unit. One can equalise the amount and kind of books and teachers' time each pupil receives. Or, for a given behavioural or learning objective, these inputs can be varied and given in unequal quantities for different pupils. For instance, teachers' time may be diverted from the bright pupils towards those who are less bright. The units of comparison can be enlarged to socio-economic groups (households, ethnic groups), demographic aggregates (sex group, age group etc.) and socio-political units (villages, towns, provinces or regions).

From the input side judgements can be made on equality in the provision of educational services to individuals, as well as to larger units such as the socio-economic groups and other aggregates we mentioned. Alternatively, it is also possible, even if more difficult, to make judgements in terms of learning outcomes and their approximations. These judgements, however, are dependent on agreed norms or standards which are yet to be either technically determined or politically established.

Given the two reference points, i.e. (a) inputs or results and (b) units of comparison, one can nibble at the edges of educational equality by citing parity of units in terms of basic skills such as literacy and numeracy. In the same fashion other gross measures of results (e.g. proportions of specified groups receiving or completing primary schooling, or attaining higher levels) may be applied. Less crude measures such as test results (e.g. school entry examinations) are also useful for judging parity (or disparity) in education.

For the purposes of this study, deviations from parity are identified as disparity or an indication of educational inequality, especially so if the size of the deviation is statistically significant.

In addition we must be clear on the limits to the scope of education. Education consists partly of schooling and partly of non-formal training and the learning events that occur in informal circumstances. Only in the abstract sense are these categories mutually exclusive: in the real world they overlap and interact, so that it is extremely difficult to isolate what might be called the 'pure' effects of schooling on learning outcomes, and later on such indirect consequences as employment and

Equality in Education 17

changes in earning streams.

This study deals mainly with schooling strictly defined, even if much of what is discussed also applies to other modes of education. The reasons for this emphasis are first that because of data availability schooling is a convenient starting point for any systematic inquiry, and secondly that formal schooling is an instrument which stands, in principle, at the ready disposal of governments.

Education narrowly defined as learning reflects mainly the process of developing abilities. More specifically, we want to approach the substantive aspects of learning, i.e. the learning outcomes. In this context education is viewed as ability creation and thus as the immediate output of learning events — whether in school, at home or anywhere else.

Learning outcomes are capable of categorisation although the variety of human abilities which are learned is probably infinite. The task of specifying and describing them is extremely involved. Rather than tinker with individual abilities, we prefer to deal with ability sets. As classified by Bloom,[4] these abilities are in three domains, namely (a) cognitive or mental ability, (b) affective states, i.e. attitudes, aspirations, values etc., and (c) psychomotor skills, or what are more popularly known as the manipulative skills. Various levels of the first two categories are well described by Bloom and Krathwohl.[5] Cognitive ability is simply thinking ability. At its initial level it is simple recall of bits of information; as such it belongs to the knowledge (or functional information) level. The next step is that of comprehension: this means that the items of information are associated and their connection is grasped.[6] These cognitive effects are the raw materials for the higher mental processes such as analysis and synthesis. Affective states are commonly referred to as attitudes and their correlates such as interests, opinions, beliefs and values. In its simple form, an attitude is merely an awareness of a stimulus without the production of any active reaction. At the complex level it involves value formation and a commitment to solve problems which require action.

In empirical work, these ability sets are measured in various ways. General mental ability, for instance, is measured (however crudely) by IQ tests; cognitive achievement in particular subject areas is evaluated by test batteries such as those used by the International Educational Achievement Association (IEA) and by college admission boards. In the affective domain, attitudes are also measured in many ways, e.g. by questionnaire, 'opinionnaire' or notation of semantic differences. Attitudes towards persons are documents by sociometric methods.

Performance tests relating to particular psychomotor skills are also available.

Effect of Schools and Other Variables

Closely related to these ability sets is the question of the extent to which schools affect learning outcomes. Popular belief sees schools as specialised institutions for ability formation. And educationalists would say that by skilfully structuring the learning process through curricula and teaching methodology, certain ability sets are developed better than others. For instance, vocational training, especially of the routine mechanical sort, tends to develop psychomotor skills better than cognitive (mental) abilities. In the cognitive domain rote teaching emphasises simple recall rather than the ability to analyse and synthesise. Freire's pedagogic method[7] has been reported to inculcate a keen awareness of relative deprivation as well as certain kinds of value orientation, outcomes which are largely in the affective domain. Adults or children acquire these ability sets at school as well as in other places. The home, market-place, church, workshop, farm or factory constitute a range of learning environments and may complement or supplement that of the school. As measured, these abilities rarely reflect what has been learned entirely from school, but from all learning environments. Nor is any of these abilities highly developed in isolation; they are developed in combinations or patterns falling in all three of the main categories distinguished above.

Now we turn to what other researchers say about the influence of schools on learned abilities, especially on those which are ostensibly taught in schools. Like Illich,[8] Jencks and Brown[9] have little faith in the effectiveness of schools. They found that

> Some high schools are more effective than others in raising test scores, and schools that boost performance on one test are not especially likely to boost performance on other tests. Moreover, high school characteristics such as social composition, per pupil expenditure, teacher training, teacher experience, and class size have no consistent impact on cognitive growth between ninth and twelfth grades . . . Similarly, some high schools are more effective than others in boosting a student's eventual educational attainment . . .
>
> However, a high school's effect on individual educational attainment does depend on social composition, but not in a simple way.

This finding sheds an unfavourable light on conventional wisdom and suggests that there is little advantage to be derived from policies of re-allocating resources to reduce differences in school characteristics.[10] Nevertheless, two other authors[11] reported that school inputs are productive. They analysed data from the Michigan Assessment Program, using new criteria. Briefly stated, their argument was as follows:

> Many previous economic studies have concluded that school inputs do not matter because mean school output is often uncorrelated with input variations. But if every student's performance matters to a school, then productive inputs affect the entire distribution of student performances. If that distribution can be characterised by its mean and variance, then inputs are productive if either moment is affected.

However, schools do not exist in a vacuum. Their productivity seems to be dependent on what the students already have: previous schooling, and especially home background, have been found to be dominant variables in scholastic achievement. For instance, Alexander and Simmons,[12] after a comprehensive review of published material on determinants of school achievement, observe that

> The consensus of findings from both developed and developing countries is that the student's socio-economic background is the major determinant of his economic achievement throughout all levels of schooling, except the upper secondary grades. *Its contribution is smaller in the developed countries, while the contribution of some schooling variables to achievement is larger in the developing countries in several subjects like science.*[13]

Moreover, it would seem that schools have a larger relative effect on measured achievement when learning opportunities at home are meagre — as is generally the case in developing countries.

Thus far, we have discussed scholastic achievement in a general sense. The findings we report refer mainly to school subjects which have a high cognitive content, e.g. science and reading. Test scores in those subjects can be shown to have systematically varied with home background, school and other factors. Results in a subject with a relatively high affective content such as civic education show a similar pattern. The cognitive element of the subject seems to elicit observations parallel to those made with regard to science and reading. Torney *et al.* report that 'home background factors . . . and word knowledge make considerably more contribution to predicting the variance in civic education cognitive achievement than do either of the affective civic outcomes'.[14] They also argue that students' 'intelligence and their command of language are both relevant to their grasp of political attitudes'.[15]

What all the foregoing results tell us is forcefully summarised by the following conclusion drawn from an inquiry into reading comprehension:

> differences in home and environmental backgrounds provide strong differentiation [in test scores] between countries and, within countries, between schools and between students.[16]

Axioms

Given the foregoing empirical explanation of why learning outcomes vary (in relation to supposed causal variables), we now turn to inferences as to why the distribution of learning outcomes varies from one individual or socio-economic group or other aggregate to another.

The first axiom is that equals added to unequals are unequal. Thus if two identical machines with the same rated capacity were given equal inputs, the chances are that their outputs would be equal. If these machines were analogous to persons with the same learning capacity (however this is measured), the expectation is that their output in terms of amount of materials learned (or skills developed) would be equal. This expectation immediately runs counter to a universally held psychological postulate which holds that no two individuals are exactly alike. Few would argue against the common observation that some persons learn faster than others, and that some can learn languages faster than prove mathematical theorems. What these observations suggest is that individuals are different and are unequal in one dimension of ability or another.

Even for persons with the same endowment, e.g. identical twins, differences in training and environment do contribute towards significant differences in ability to learn, among other individual traits.[17] The slums of Calcutta and of Tondo, Manila, and the palatial homes of modern maharajahs tell of yawning gaps in environment; the brisk tempo of a metropolis and the tarry-a-while life in rural areas also tell the same story; the disparities between computer-equipped city schools

Equality in Education

and schools without books in villages would affect educational performances. Given these disparities in environment, is equalising the input of educational resources into schools likely to equalise results?

Studies on determinants affecting scholastic achievement (mentioned earlier) indicate that pupils coming from better-endowed homes and communities tend to perform better.[18] These reports seem to give an impression that the effect of better previous training and environment on learning ability might be multiplicative rather than additive. If indeed this is so, then equalising of inputs in school would produce widely different results.

It also remains generally true that unequals added to unequals are unequal. This axiom is false only when the first quantity is compensatory, i.e. sufficient to make the results equal.

That individuals are different and by implication unequal in learning ability was postulated earlier. When individuals are exposed to unequal amounts of educational resources, the results would be somewhat uncertain. However, it is useful to isolate two possibilities: (a) allocating more and better resources to bright individuals than to the less bright, and (b) providing more resources to the less bright than to the brighter ones. In the first case the results would tend to be unequal (in fact widely unequal); in the second, the tendency is towards equality.

What happens in reality is that the allocation of educational resources tends to be towards those who already have educational advantages, i.e. to the brighter students and to those coming from high-income families. Admission examinations, special schools for the gifted and exclusive schools are only a few devices that sort out people who are to receive more and better educational services. From the systematic co-variation between certain variables and scholastic achievement, it can be inferred that whatever the resources that are provided to schools, pupils with better home backgrounds tend to benefit more from them than pupils of humbler origins. If this inference is true, then the implication is that as resources are allocated towards children with better backgrounds, scholastic achievement will diverge sharply, even for the same number of years spent at school.

Where compensatory allocations of educational resources are made in an attempt to benefit the less fortunate, the attempt is usually a stopgap measure taken only when inequalities are so wide that they are difficult and very expensive to remedy. Examples of this include Project Head Start[19] and related anti-poverty programmes in the United States.

Schools therefore produce different kinds of abilities — cognitive,

22 *Equality in Education*

affective and psychomotor skills — and they produce them more rapidly and efficiently for children from certain kinds of background. But there are further complications. To reach higher levels of education, not only does a child need the ability to perform well in selective tests and examinations but its family also needs the staying power to keep the child in school, or to convince the child that persistence in the educational system is worth while. A family's resources, whether in money, in land or in some other form, are obviously relevant here to the extent that they determine whether the household can go without the income contribution of the children. In addition, the household's appraisal of the prospects for social mobility is important. If many households see the main function of schooling as providing a kind of 'baby-sitting' service which also teaches a rudimentary knowledge of the three Rs, then the education system will not be a very effective redistributive instrument, however defined.

Abilities and Productivity

We have seen that schools are likely to produce very unequal patterns of learning outcomes and abilities in different persons. Furthermore, once developed, the three different ability sets we mentioned (cognitive, affective and psychomotor skills) are likely to have widely different effects on the individual's later economic productivity and efficiency. Above all, jobs requiring mental skills, for which cognitive abilities are highly developed, are universally better rewarded, in pay and status, than jobs requiring largely manual and psychomotor skills. Nor is the ability-productivity link reserved solely for the job market. Sound decision-making for allocative efficiency posits a certain level of mental ability. This is seen in studies which show that the more educated households (where we would expect cognitive skills to be more developed than psychomotor skills) tend to make a better choice (than less educated households) of means of achieving

(a) total health of the family, reduction of morbidity and mortality, and increase in the family's labour availability;[20]
(b) fertility control and sound upbringing of children;[21]
(c) efficient use of new seeds and fertiliser for the farm;[22]
(d) the sound choice of goods and services to meet basic needs.

One further productive and highly valued outcome of the develop-

Equality in Education

ment of different ability sets concerns 'learning to learn', again a product of cognitive and, perhaps, affective abilities. 'Learning to learn' describes broadly the capacity to adjust to new situations and to cope efficiently with external changes and developments. In changing situations the ability to consider adjustments requires good mental capability and a willingness to change; people who do not change tend to fall behind. This principle does not refer solely to a few well-paid jobs requiring a very high level of mental complexity; it refers equally to small farmers who investigate and use new techniques of production, to migrants, to job-seekers or to factory workers. Educational outcomes which diminish the development of cognitive abilities for such groups and stress the development of psychomotor skills may affect their future unfavourably.

Notes

1. C.A. Anderson and M.J. Bowman, 'Theoretical Issues in Educational Planning' in M. Blaug (ed.), *Economics of Education* (Harmondsworth, Penguin Books, 1968).

2. Throughout this study we assume that innate abilities are randomly distributed among individuals.

3. See C. Seshadri, 'Equality of Educational Opportunity: Some Issues in Indian Education', *Comparative Education*, Vol. 12 (October 1976), pp. 219-29.

4. Benjamin S. Bloom (ed.), *Taxonomy of Educational Objectives. Handbook I: Cognitive Domain* (New York, Longmans, Green and Co., 1956).

5. David R. Krathwohl et al., *Taxonomy of Educational Objectives. Handbook II: Affective Domain* (New York, David McKay, 1964).

6. The next level is an active use of functional information and comprehension, and is called 'application'. Its sophisticated form may utilise the higher mental processes.

7. Paulo Freire, *Education for Critical Consciousness* (New York, Seabury Press, 1973).

8. I.D. Illich, *Deschooling Society* (London, Calder and Boyars, 1971).

9. Christopher S. Jencks and Marsha D. Brown, 'Effects of High Schools on their Students', *Harvard Educational Review*, Vol. 45 (August 1975), pp. 320ff.

10. Our attention has been drawn to a recent advance in multivariate analysis which shows that the effect of schools on cognitive achievement has been seriously underestimated by previous research using classical regression analysis. See Richard Noonan and Herman Wold, 'Nipals Path Modelling with Latent Variables', *Scandinavian Journal of Educational Research*, Vol. 21 (1977), pp. 33-61. An application of the Nipals technique to Botswana data demonstrated the importance of school variables such as teacher quality.

11. Byron W. Brown and Daniel H. Saks, 'The Production and Distribution of Cognitive Skills Within Schools', *Journal of Political Economy*, Vol. 83 (June 1975), p. 571.

12. Leigh Alexander and John Simmons, *The Determinants of School Achievement in Developing Countries — The Educational Production Function*, Staff

Working Paper No. 201, International Bank for Reconstruction and Development, March 1975.

13. Our emphasis.

14. Judith V. Torney et al., *Civic Education in Ten Countries*, International Studies in Evaluation VI (Stockholm, Almquist and Wiksell, 1975), p. 326.

15. Ibid., p. 19; however, the authors further asserted, 'knowledge [of civics] does not correlate highly with support for democratic values, even less as children get older . . . Neither does this knowledge . . . correlate highly with various measures of political participation.'

16. D.A. Walker, *The IEA Six-Subject Survey — An Empirical Study of Education in Twenty-One Countries*, International Studies in Evaluation IX (Stockholm, Almquist and Wiksell, 1975), p. 121.

17. C.O. Carter, 'The Genetic Basis of Inequality' in A.B. Atkinson (ed.), *The Economics of Inequality* (Oxford, Clarendon Press, 1975). See also P. Taubman, 'Personal Characteristics and the Distribution of Earnings' in Atkinson, pp. 139-226.

18. See Harold S. Beebout, 'The Production Surface for Academic Achievement: An Economic Study of Malaysian Secondary Schools', unpublished PhD thesis, University of Wisconsin, 1972. See also Alexander and Simmons, *Determinants of School Achievement*.

19. See Roger Lewin, 'Head Start Pays Off', *New Scientist* (3 March 1977), pp. 508f.

20. Michael Grossman, *The Demand for Health: A Theoretical and Empirical Investigation* (New York, National Bureau of Economic Research, 1972). See also Robert T. Michael, *The Effect of Education on Efficiency in Consumption* (New York, National Bureau of Economic Research, 1972).

21. See, for example, Robert T. Michael, 'Education and the Derived Demand for Children' in T.W. Schultz (ed.), *Economics of the Family* (Chicago, University of Chicago Press, 1974), pp. 120-56.

22. Finis Welch, 'Education in Production', *Journal of Political Economy*, Vol. 78 (January-February 1970), pp. 35-9. The subject is also dealt with in the following two mimeographed ILO World Employment Programme research working papers (restricted): D.P. Chaudhri, *Effect of Farmer's Education on Agricultural Productivity and Employment — A Case Study of Punjab and Haryana States of India (1960-1972)* (Geneva, ILO, 1974); M.D. Leonor Jr, *Education and Productivity: Some Evidence and Implications* (Geneva, ILO, 1976).

2 SCHOOLING, EARNINGS AND OCCUPATION

In the previous chapter we reviewed some concepts of equality in education and their meanings. In this chapter we examine the broad picture of the effect of education on the labour market. We start by summarising some evidence on the relation of educational achievement to earnings in Asia. We then discuss some broad issues concerning the link between education and income distribution. In a third section we discuss the process by which new educated groups enter the labour market and the way in which that market reacts. All these issues are treated briefly as an introduction to the more empirical work which is discussed in following chapters. A final section in this chapter presents data on recent overall trends in Asia both in educational expansion and in employment.

Education and Earnings

Evidence that education is a productive asset can be taken from many sources. Regression analyses of groups of workers show that in Bangkok, for example, an extra year of schooling was associated with earnings that were 11 per cent higher for men and 15 per cent higher for women after controlling for age.[1] Data for Malaysia (urban males only) show increases ranging from 7 to 11 per cent according to ethnic group.[2] Very rarely (only for some degree courses in the Philippines) do available sources show negligible rates of return.[3] Rates of return — particularly in this context private rates of return — are generally high. Thus for West Malaysia, Hoerr found average private rates of return of 13 per cent for primary education and 17 per cent for secondary education, controlling for rural-urban location.[4] Marginal rates for secondary education were higher. Blaug found marginal private rates of return to investment in education in Bangkok of 24 per cent for primary education and 11 per cent thereafter.[5] These high private rates of return naturally include the effects of less than full cost pricing, or indeed of 100 per cent subsidies for educational services. However, in terms of the income redistribution objectives of educational policy, the virtue of educational programmes would lie precisely in the fact that permanent and reliable income-earning assets could be created through a fiscal transfer or subsidy.

Education generally interacts with age in influencing earnings, as Table 2.1 shows. The table gives data for the USA contrasted with survey data for Sri Lanka. In the USA, earnings on average rise steeply with level of education (i.e. reading down the columns) but much more so for the older than the younger age groups. On average, also, the distribution of earnings within any educational category (here measured simply by the relation of the mean to the median) becomes more unequal with age, particularly for the older age group with college education. The Sri Lanka data are based on a sample survey, and the absolute numbers in some of the cells are very small. However, the general pattern is fairly close to that observed for the USA: earnings increase with age, and the higher the level of education the greater the increase is; the same general pattern of a widening dispersion of earnings with age can be observed, with the greatest dispersion for the oldest and most educated professional workers. These data are, of course, taken from a cross-section and not from a longitudinal study. Some of the extra earnings associated with age may reflect an advantage gained in youth when higher education was more scarce. It is our contention, however, that scarcity in higher levels of education (and, above all, inequality in the distribution of educational outputs) will be a feature of Asian economies for a very long time.

Table 2.1: Male* Earnings by Age and Education in the USA and Sri Lanka, 1969

Level of education in the USA and Sri Lanka	Age		Per cent change with age	Ratio (median: mean) at age	
	25-34	55-64		25-34	55-64
Elementary	100	100	9.3	0.96	0.96
Primary	*100*	*100*	*3.9*	*0.81*	*0.74*
High school (4 years)	138	146	15.2	0.99	0.91
Middle school	*151*	*162*	*11.4*	*0.95*	*0.85*
College (5 years)	184	294	75.0	0.95	0.79
Graduate	*264*	*496*	*95.3*	*0.91*	*0.75*

*All male workers. Data for female workers' earnings are available for the USA. For the older age group their performance is very similar to that of male workers. However, the increase with education for the younger age group is far (about three times) greater than for males. Correspondingly, the increase with age for the elementary school group is far higher than for males, some 90 per cent. For the college group it is some 60 per cent.

Sources: USA: *Earnings by Occupation and Education* (US Department of Commerce) and 1970 census of population; Sri Lanka: *Socio-Economic Survey* (Department of Census and Statistics, 1969-70, Colombo).

One can thus be fairly confident that the same general pattern of interaction between age and education level will broadly reappear in any wage-employed labour market. Thus Anand's study on Malaysia shows both age and years of education bringing a greater reward for professional than for factory workers: an extra year of education is associated with an additional 13 per cent of income for professional workers and 4-5 per cent for factory workers, whereas a year of age added 6 per cent and 4 per cent respectively to incomes. What needs to be mentioned at this stage, however, is that the occupations with, on this reckoning, the highest reward for education have already a uniformly high level of education, and the greatest bunching of educational levels.

Granted the empirical proposition that in wage labour markets earnings do vary with level of education, that age has different effects depending on different levels of education, and that age and education interact differently in different occupations, one can ask why all this happens. If it were true that education is an income-earning asset which is completely divisible and could be spread among individuals at the whim of the educational authorities, it should also bring a reward to the self-employed. We have already noted that productivity increases for the self-employed are likely to require the development of improved allocative efficiency in business: certainly it seems likely that not all educational outcomes will guarantee this.

Education, Occupations and Income Distribution

We have noted the links between education, ability creation and productivity, but we would certainly not wish to imply that these links totally explained the education-occupation-income relation discussed in the last section. In Asia nearly all highly educated people (professional, managerial and clerical workers) and most of the moderately educated (production and service workers) are in wage employment. The theories of education-occupation linkage in wage employment are very diverse.[6] Some refer to the social and home background of individuals who are most 'successful' in the educational system and who would obtain the best jobs anyway in a relatively immobile class-structured society, whereas other theories relate to workers who automatically do well in jobs, because employers, seeing their lauded (but perhaps completely irrelevant) school performance, give them the chance to do well. Of course, one perfectly good explanation is that some of the skills provided by systems of education do correspond to the requirements for contributing most in a subsequent wage employment.

From the point of view of income distribution policy there are perhaps three extreme interpretations of the relationship:

(a) Educational systems are only reproducing, or perhaps slightly altering, the current structure of society: the best jobs go therefore to the descendants of certain families.
(b) Educational systems and overall income distribution are both determined by the job structure of the economy, which only changes slowly; whatever the average levels of educational investment and achievement, there would still be the same rules relating educational performance to jobs.
(c) Educational systems can be so manipulated by governments that resources can be directed towards the poor and can be used to increase their earning power.

It can be noted that (b) is quite compatible with equality of educational opportunity and with a situation in which the children of poorer households would win access to the highest-paying jobs. Proposition (c) is compatible with proposition (a), on the assumption that governments are unwilling to direct more resources towards the poor. In conjunction with proposition (b), however, proposition (c) implies that any occupation can profitably absorb more education, and that therefore occupation-income linkages could change. Proposition (b) suggests that inflation in educational qualifications could go on indefinitely. As we shall see, there is considerable evidence for proposition (a), given the greater educational success, both in terms of years of attendance and of abilities created, of children of the rich.

Proposition (b) leads to the common hypothesis of 'bumping', i.e. that the more educated move into occupations previously held by the less educated. There are different versions of this hypothesis: one allows the reward for the education of the more educated to remain high, even when they are downgraded occupationally, while the reward for the less educated tends to fall; the other sees greater strength in occupational than in educational differentials.

In a sense the third hypothesis is the most important, since it implies that a conventional educational system could be used to bring about a radical redistribution of income. This would be done by changing the distribution of education outcomes, not only by redirecting them towards the poor but by making their variation less extreme. This is certainly

Schooling, Earnings and Occupation

what many policy-makers would like to believe. In fact, however, during the 1960s the distribution of years of education would hardly seem to have changed in the two countries for which we have evidence, viz. the Philippines and Sri Lanka. This could be evidence that education does confer valuable income-earning assets wherever used, and that various groups in society are fighting each other to get them. However, it could equally well be the effect of inherited poverty, lethargy or lack of confidence in education for some groups and awareness of the value of education as a credential, particularly in wage employment, for other groups.

Partly it is the widespread use of rates of return to education which gives the impression that an educational system could be used in a relatively painless manner to readjust income distribution. Rates of return, of course, relate future earnings to costs of education (largely teachers' salaries) and the individual's income foregone. Since income foregone is likely to be directly related to the income inequality of an economy, the greater the income inequality, the lower, relatively, will be income foregone compared to future income, and thus the higher the rate of return. Given subsidised education, income inequality itself creates a demand for education. Naturally this leads to the suspicion that rates of return to human capital created through education are high when (a) differences in occupational incomes are high and (b) the occupation-education link is close. As a result it would be misleading to think of human capital as being exchangeable for physical capital on an equal level, based on the costs involved. Human capital is no doubt a substitute for physical capital, but the rate of substitution varies.

How then can one expect an education system to assist in altering the overall distribution of income? A number of answers are possible.

(a) Within an unchanged distribution of educational achievement and unchanged distribution of jobs and of personal earnings from work, the educational structure could promote social mobility. As a result, savings and other forms of capital formation permitted by high-wage incomes would accrue to different families in different generations. This effect may be all the more important in developing countries where the existence of wide variations in the quality of primary education probably restricts the efficiency of the educational system in selecting all children of ability.
(b) An attempt could be made to move the educational system much more quickly towards the equalisation of educational achievement. This will not happen if the educational system responds to the

demands of various occupations for recruits of a certain level of education, frequently a rising one. Inequality of educational achievement is built into the labour market structure and has become a necessary condition for the labour market to continue to function in the usual way.

With such a pattern, moves towards equality, even in terms of years of education, will probably take a century to be effective, since the educational appetite of the higher occupations must first be satisfied. To move towards any significant level of equal education, quickly, will require a shift of resources from the top to the bottom of the education system and a restriction of access to education at certain levels. However, the fundamental point to be faced here is that even perfect equality of educational outcomes would have its costs and benefits. Since social status is closely tied up with educational status there can be little doubt that previously uninfluential groups at the bottom of the occupational hierarchy would receive a considerable boost to their confidence, although perhaps not to their power. On the other hand, with no educational inequality, employers would be deprived of the use of educational outcomes as a screening and certifying device, yet would still want some means of selecting recruits. It is not obvious that whatever alternative they discovered would work in favour of the poor.

It can also be pointed out that even the equalisation of educational achievement would not equalise private rates of return to educational investment at the margin, i.e. some pupils would rationally wish to drop out earlier. Of course, the rationality of the wish might be questioned and, of course, in principle fiscal policy can be used to alter private rates of return.

(c) The educational system can be used deliberately to overproduce highly educated graduates even at the cost of worsening distribution in terms of such indicators as years of education in the short run. In the longer run such a policy might have the advantage of reducing the relative salary levels of the teaching profession and thus making education less expensive in the future. In principle the object would be to reduce once and for all the relative incomes of the higher-educated occupations. Whether such a policy is likely to achieve such an object, rather than, for example, narrow the range of incomes by educational level but simultaneously raise the average education level of higher occupations, is questionable. Such a policy may seriously misfire, and it would in any event be expensive.

(d) The content of education may be changed so as to instil more relevant cognitive and affective skills. This is an approach to which we shall return in our chapter on innovations in education. Irrelevant and

Schooling, Earnings and Occupation

unattractive content may be an important reason for early drop-outs, so that an altered curriculum may have some effect on retention rates. Of course, changed content, plus other fundamental changes in society, may lead to the acceptance of different occupation-education linkages (destroying the mutual support of educational, occupational and social status) and of different occupation-income linkages. But we doubt that this can occur.

(e) Fiscal policy can be used to alter private rates of return, either by subsidising costs to the poor or by withdrawing benefits from the rich. Such action would be an important step towards equalising access to education, and could go some way towards countering the effect of background variables on educational achievement. There are naturally problems here: taxes and subsidies will be paid or enjoyed by parents and the income stream largely by the children. However, parents are also investing in their children for their own future support. What is missing is the automatic balancing mechanism which appears in the human capital model and may apply in practice in some educational systems: this mechanism would allow individuals to borrow and to invest in their own education; future repayments would then automatically reduce their rate of return. Given that in Asian educational systems individual borrowing, although not family borrowing, is very rare, this mechanism will hardly operate. However, fiscal policy can in principle change the distribution of educational outcomes by altering family decisions on whether or not to give the children more years of education. An equitable fiscal system, in this context, will therefore be one that raises the private rates of return to education for the poor and lowers them for the rich.

Education and Entry to the Labour Market

The general discussion of the previous two sections can be rounded off with some remarks on the means by which educational expansion impinges on the labour market. Two main hypotheses have generally been used to describe the integration of new job-seekers into the labour market, those of wage competition and of job competition. There are extreme versions of both: under wage competition individuals determine their output and income by their own attributes (including education); under job competition individuals can exert no further influence on their output and income once they have been slotted into jobs. In the latter alternative, education serves as a privately cheap but socially expensive method of selecting likely and 'trainable' job candidates. According to the first hypothesis, any surplus of job-seekers in any particular educational category (as perceived by a large number of independently acting employers) will compete with each other to force down wages, which will cause an expansion of job opportunities for that group (presumably with some lag). According to the second hypothesis, the structure of jobs (and in extreme cases the structure of incomes) is independent of the number and educational characteristics of new job-seekers. However, where education is the main criterion used for job selection, the result is 'educational inflation' and the requirement of ever higher levels of formal education for an unchanged job.

Both hypotheses predict a fall in relative earnings for any surplus educational category, although this fall would be brought about in different ways. However, in the event of a surplus of candidates in a highly educated category, the job competition model predicts that members of less educated groups will also experience a relative income fall as the 'downward bumping' process takes place: that is, as the more educated overflow into jobs previously held by the less educated. The contrast between the two hypotheses can be exaggerated. Presumably under the wage competition model some change in the nature of the jobs done by the surplus group takes place, and if it does not take place at the same rate for everyone it may appear as a change in occupations. Conversely, the job competition model must allow for some personal attributes to play a role, for example, in promotion. In practice the validity of both hypotheses depends greatly on the speed at which technological change takes place; presumably the faster the rate of change, the greater will be the spread of 'jobs' for any educational category and the more varied the ways in which age, education and occupation can interact.

Neither approach was expressly designed for the labour market problems of developing countries, and neither would appear to take explicit account of educated unemployment, the major position of governments as employers and the large share of self-employment. The last point means that access to other resources (capital or land) through a family business can be as important as education in setting a person up in secure and well-rewarded employment.

In Asia, one must take account of the major role of governments as employers, particularly of the educated. The advantages of employment in the public sector very frequently repay the cost of waiting for jobs to come free, or of undergoing a long selection process. This itself

Schooling, Earnings and Occupation

can be one explanation for the educated unemployment in many Asian market economies. But the role of the public sector has other effects. As an employer, the government can be expected to have a relatively inflexible attitude towards wage differentials, so that its behaviour is likely to tend towards a job competition model. Furthermore, in the interests of impartiality it is likely to prefer the use of educational achievement as a selection mechanism. Once this is fully recognised within a country, the struggle for the best jobs is pushed back within the education system.

Educated unemployment may have one other major explanation, that of mismatch or of unwillingness either to force wages downwards by competition (which may be impossible) or to accept undesirable lower-status jobs. The waiting period of unemployment then results either in an attitudinal change and the acceptance of less desirable employment, or in a later start in the desired occupation. However, little is known about this supposed attitudinal change and who generally must bear its costs.

Recent Educational Expansion and Employment Change in Asia

The phenomenal rate of expansion of Asian educational systems is well known. During the 1960s the number of pupils at the various levels grew at rates clustering around 5-8 per cent (according to the country) for primary education, 7-12 per cent for secondary and 10-15 per cent for tertiary. Public expenditure on education as a share of the gross national product often ranges around 2.5 to 4.5 per cent, and UNESCO has predicted an average for total educational costs (not including income foregone) of over 5 per cent for the more highly educated Asian countries by 1980.[7] Systems vary: some of this cost will be taken up privately, but the bulk will remain a government responsibility. Education is therefore the largest single programme that many governments run.

Table 2.2 brings out another aspect of the recent increase in educational expansion. It shows an increase in all the countries cited of school enrolment[8] of teenagers, or at least of those aged 14-17, before anything approaching full enrolment has been achieved at the primary level, except in one instance (the exception is Hong Kong): indeed, primary school enrolment may even be stagnating at around the 80 per cent mark in some countries. Full confidence cannot be given to the data in Table 2.2, but they do suggest two possibilities. One would be a desire that is quite widely expressed within educational systems, irrespective of whether it is shared or resented by educational planners, that primary education should take second place. The other is the existence of a group of families, presumably among the very poor, who do not consider education to be very important for their children, or who are prevented from doing so.

Table 2.2: School Enrolment in Selected Asian Countries

Country	Source	Year	Percentage of age group		
			6-12	6-13	14-17
Thailand	UNESCO	1961	70.9	65.4	13.5
	UNESCO	1968	69.3	63.6	13.2
	Census	1970	65.4	61.5	17.1
Sri Lanka	UNESCO	1961	78.2	76.6	n.a.
	UNESCO	1967	76.5	73.1	40.7
	Min. Ed.	1969	78.6	76.6	41.2
Philippines	UNESCO	1967	77.0	74.4	25.6
	Census	1970	61.6	63.1	50.0
West Malaysia	UNESCO	1960	66.3	63.2	18.2
	UNESCO	1967	79.9*	74.4	18.8
South Korea	UNESCO	1963	86.5	81.4	18.3
	UNESCO	1970	86.0	81.1	39.1
India	UNESCO	1965	53.6	50.2	17.1
	UNICEF	1970	79.1 (6-11)	–	20.2
Hong Kong	UNESCO	1960	66.0	63.7	36.8
	UNESCO	1969	83.9	82.0	61.0
	Census	1971	94.7	98.3	63.4 (14-16 only)

*By 1967 most children were entering school at the age of 6, and not 7 as in 1961.
Key: UNESCO = UNESCO, *Statistical Yearbook*, various issues.
UNICEF = UNICEF (New Delhi), *Statistical Profile of Children and Youth in India*, June 1972.
Census = most recent national census.

It is hardly safe to generalise further about Asian educational systems. The variations in tertiary education are immense. At the end of the 1960s two countries of a similar population size, the Philippines and Thailand, had respectively 630,000 and 42,000 students in third-level education. In the middle 1960s India had over a million and Sri Lanka around 13,000; the ratio of students to total population was twice as high in the former country by comparison with the latter. Nor can one generalise about the internal structures of the various educational systems: they have different divisions into primary and secondary, different curricular choices, different schemes of promotion and examination. However, given the largely similar nature of the economies mentioned so far, it is highly likely that education interacts with income, occupation and status in similar ways; and given a similar importance of education, it is likely that different educational systems will respond to much the same pressures in much the same ways.

Corresponding in a way to the trends forecasted in Table 2.2, trends in the educational structure of the employed labour force in a number of Asian countries can be studied. Since the labour force trends also refer to the period of the 1960s and early 1970s the effect of educational expansion in the same period cannot be followed, but if the trends portrayed in the two tables outlast the decade in question the tables can still provide a useful comparison.

Table 2.3: Educational Structure of the Labour Force in Selected Asian Countries, *circa* 1960-70

Education sector	Hong Kong	India	Philippines	Singapore	Sri Lanka	Thailand
Circa 1960						
High	25	8	17	36	17	8
Medium	70	16	28	56	32	9
Low	5	75	55	8	51	83
Whole labour force*	100	100	100	100	100	100
Circa 1970						
High	27	11	17	41	18	9
Medium	69	14	29	55	34	11
Low	3	75	54	4	48	79
Whole labour force*	100	100	100	100	100	100
Changes circa 1960-70 (%)						
High	*+11*	*+31*	*- 1*	*+ 14*	*+ 6*	*+ 16*
Medium	*- 1*	*- 15*	*+ 4*	*- 2*	*+ 3*	*+ 23*
Low	*- 38*	*—*	*- 2*	*- 46*	*- 5*	*- 4*

*Totals may not add up to 100 because of rounding.
Key: High   = workers in professional, managerial, clerical and sales occupations.
      Medium = workers in services and production occupations, other than agriculture.
      Low   = workers in agriculture.
Source: National censuses of population.

Table 2.3 shows the educational structure of the employed labour force in six Asian countries in the early 1960s and early 1970s. On the basis of occupational groups the labour force is divided into high, medium and low education sectors. As might be expected, the low sector is particularly small in Hong Kong and Singapore, but large in India and Thailand. During the period the high education sector showed a general tendency to grow faster than any other sector. There were, however, exceptions: in both the Philippines and Thailand it was the medium education sector which increased most quickly, i.e. generally workers in services and in production occupations. The most urbanised among these countries, Hong Kong and Singapore, saw very little change in their medium education sectors, a considerable fall in their low education sectors and an increase only in the high education sector. In India, on the other hand, the high education sector rose as the medium education sector fell. This presumably increased the pressure on job-seekers to find clerical and similar jobs, a pressure which must have been to some degree relieved in the Philippines and Thailand. A slow growth in the high education sector, and certainly a slow growth unrelieved by a fast rate of increase in the medium education sector, is very likely to lead to an inflation of educational qualifications for recruitment. Such an inflation is no recipe for an increase in educational equality.

Conclusion

In this chapter we have carried the discussion one stage further. We have discussed some possible interactions between education and income distribution, through occupation. We have also drawn attention to some issues that are particularly relevant for Asia: one is the prevalence of educated unemployment and its corollary, the inflation of educational qualifications (we shall meet the latter point also in the next chapter). Educated unemployment leads not to spurning education but to a thirst for higher levels of education. We have seen that educational authorities have responded to this demand by allowing a faster rise of secondary than primary school enrolment. However, the demand also leads to greater competition within the school system where, in fact, decisions on future occupations and earnings are effectively being made. Later chapters will look in detail at some factors which determine success and the distribution of achievement within the school system.

While we certainly believe that most of the major factors we have discussed, such as the relation of education to occupation and earnings, are common to the great majority of Asian countries, we recognise their differences. We have drawn attention to the different rates of expansion of various sectors of the labour markets of Asian countries; between, say, India and Thailand the differences, particularly in the rates of expansion of transport and manufacturing industries, have been very great. These different rates of expansion will no doubt lead to different income patterns. However, while the pressure exerted within the education system will no doubt be greater in some countries than others, its role in the overall process remains the same.

Notes

1. C.U. Chiswick, *The Distribution of Income in Bangkok* (International Bank for Reconstruction and Development, 1975).
2. S. Anand, *The Size Distribution of Income in Malaysia* (International Bank for Reconstruction and Development, 1973).
3. ILO, *Sharing in Development: A Programme of Employment, Equity and Growth for the Philippines* (Geneva, 1974), p. 653.
4. O.D. Hoerr, 'Education, Income and Equity in Malaysia', *Economic Development and Cultural Change* (January 1973).
5. M. Blaug, *The Rate of Return to Investment in Education in Thailand* (Bangkok, 1973). Further evidence on private rates of return to education is found in M. Blaug, *Education and the Employment Problem in Developing Countries* (Geneva, ILO, 1973).
6. See particularly R. Dore, *Human Capital Theory, the Diversity of Societies and the Problem of Quality in Education* (mimeographed).
7. United Nations, *Economic Survey of Asia and the Far East, 1973* (Bangkok, 1974), Part One: 'Education and Employment', p. 54, Table I-4-16.
8. Governments generally collect enrolment data from within the school system. Such information may be biased upwards. A census or survey is more likely to ask whether a child normally attends school, or attended during the reference period.

3 EDUCATIONAL EXPANSION AND THE LABOUR MARKET

The purpose of this chapter is to investigate the effect of educational expansion on the labour market. The bulk of the analysis is restricted to the Philippines and Sri Lanka although, again, some comparisons are made with the USA. We discuss the change in the average number of years of education received by members of the labour force, the distribution of those years of education and their relation to particular occupations. We also review changes in relative incomes in different occupations and in unemployment rates. As already stated, the number of years of education received is far from adequate as a measure of education. However, it is at present the only unit of measurement available for purposes of international comparison and indeed for the assessment of distribution. But, as we shall discuss in later chapters, it must not be assumed that an equal number of years of education, nor, indeed, obtaining the same certificates, will develop the same level of abilities.

Most of the data used in this chapter relate to both male and female workers, without distinction; it is impossible to make separate analyses for each sex since income data are not available by sex. However, where the share of each sex in a particular occupation seems to have changed significantly or where the age composition of an occupational group seems to have been affected by a change in its sex composition, reference will be made to the change.

Years of Education and the Labour Market

The first step is to estimate the average amount of education, measured in years, and to investigate the extent of its change during the 1960s — the only period for which reliable census information is at hand. Particularly for Sri Lanka, this requires estimates of the years of education associated with certain examinations and certificates. The average number of years of education of the employed labour force, measured independently of occupation or income, rose in Sri Lanka (from 1963 to 1971, or over the intercensal period) from 4.8 to 5.4. In the Philippines the rise was from 6.1 to 6.5 years. If the unemployed were included these figures would change as follows: Sri Lanka

Educational Expansion and the Labour Market

5 to 5.8 years; the Philippines 6.3 to 6.6 years. The unemployed are therefore more educated than the average worker in both countries, although they are coming closer to the average in the Philippines and moving further from it in Sri Lanka.

If we calculate Gini coefficients for the distribution of years of education for all the employed (which is justified if we consider these years of education as assets) it appears that in Sri Lanka the coefficients fell from .43 to .39 over the intercensal period. In the Philippines there was a fall from .39 to .36. On this count, years of education are already more evenly spread in the Philippines, unlike incomes, which are not. However, when the distribution is recalculated to take account not of the years of education but of 'investment units' (i.e. of total costs involved), the ranking of the two countries changes. The Gini coefficient for the Philippines falls from .62 to .6 and for Sri Lanka from .5 to .47. The transformation of years of education into investment units, which take account of all costs plus income foregone for the various years of education, was made using national scales, on a different basis for the two countries, since the relative costs of education at different levels vary between the two countries. In each country both the distribution of investment in education within the labour force and the distribution of years of education improved to a very slight extent.

For Sri Lanka, it is possible to construct a table (Table 3.1) which shows how total years of education were spread between three categories of persons, the employed, the unemployed and those outside the labour force. In terms of educational investment units, 10 percentage points less were used in employment at the end of the period and fully 6 percentage points more had been accumulated by persons outside the labour force entirely. In Hong Kong, by contrast, some 71 per cent of years of education were in the employed labour force in 1971, as compared with 49 per cent in Sri Lanka. Different rates of unemployment are important in this comparison, although the far higher share of educated women in Sri Lanka who are outside the labour force makes the major difference.

The next step is to find out where in the labour market the additional education produced was used. Tables 3.2 and 3.3 show for the Philippines and Sri Lanka the breakdown of the employed by major occupation, their average number of years of education, and the distribution of years of education and of investment units among occupations. The two tables show not dissimilar occupational breakdowns, although some changes during the 1960s were more pronounced in one country than the other. They show that, as might be expected from the

40 *Educational Expansion and the Labour Market*

Table 3.1: Distribution of Education by Employment Status in Sri Lanka, 1963 and 1971

Category of persons by employment status	Proportion of population aged 15 plus		Average no. of years of education		Proportion of total number of years of education		Proportion of total number of investment units	
	1963	1971	1963	1971	1963	1971	1963	1971
Employed	56.5	50.0	4.8	5.4	57.7	48.9	58.1	48.2
Unemployed	4.8	6.6	6.8	8.7	6.9	10.4	8.0	11.8
Others	38.7	43.4	4.3	5.2	35.4	40.8	33.8	39.8
All*	100.0	100.0	4.7	5.5	100.0	100.0	100.0	100.0

*Figures may not add up to 100 because of rounding.
Source: Department of Census and Statistics, *Census of Population,* 1963 and 1971.

overall higher average, the Philippines has somewhat higher average educational levels for all occupations. In terms of educational investment units both countries showed a fall in the share accruing to the agricultural labour force and an increase for the clerical labour force during the intercensal period.

It is, above all, useful to look at the last four columns of the tables, relating the share of the labour force to the share of total number of years of education and to the share of educational investment. For columns 11 and 12, the greater range of the Philippines data reflects a different method of calculating investment units, plus a higher absolute number of years of education. These ratios of investment to labour force show considerable stability. However, it is notable that in Sri Lanka, even on this basis, the share of educational investment received by agricultural workers fell in relation to the average. As regards the ratio of years of education to labour force (columns 9 and 10) the first observation to be made is that the data for the two countries are very similar. The ranking of various occupations in terms of the average number of years of education is almost identical. Presumably this reflects the interaction of educational status and occupational status in relatively market-oriented economies. It is also interesting to note that the ratios hardly changed although the relative position of agricultural workers in Sri Lanka fell. And this was despite an increase in years of education by over six months overall, and a considerable relative decrease in the number of years of education of people in productive employment.

Since certain occupations would seem to be able to exert pressure to

Table 3.2: Distribution of Education by Occupation in the Philippines, circa 1960 and 1970

Occupations	Proportion of labour force		Average no. of years of education		Proportion of total number of years of education		Distribution of educational investment units		(5)/(1)	(6)/(2)	(7)/(1)	(8)/(1)
	c. 1960 (1)	1970 (2)	c. 1960 (3)	1970 (4)	c. 1960 (5)	1970 (6)	c. 1960 (7)	1970 (8)	(9)	(10)	(11)	(12)
Professional	5.5	5.7	14.1	14.3	12.8	12.6	33.1	31.7	2.3 ⎤	2.2 ⎤	6.0 ⎤	5.6 ⎤
Administrative	1.4	1.2	9.8	10.3	2.3	1.9	3.4	2.9	1.6 ⎦ −2.2	1.6 ⎦ −2.1	2.4 ⎦ −5.3	2.4 ⎦ −5.0
Clerical	2.9	3.3	12.6	12.9	6.0	6.6	12.8	14.3	2.1	2.0	4.4	4.3
Sales	7.5	6.9	7.0	7.5	8.7	8.0	5.6	6.2	1.2	1.2	0.7	0.9
Agriculture	54.8	53.9	4.3	4.7	38.8	39.0	24.9	24.2	0.7	0.7	0.4	0.4
Production	22.3	21.3	6.8	7.2	25.2	23.7	16.2	15.7	1.1	1.1	0.7	0.7
Services	5.5	7.7	6.7	6.8	6.2	8.2	3.9	5.1	1.1	1.1	0.7	0.7
All	100.0	100.0	6.1	6.5	100.0	100.0	100.0	100.0	1.0	1.0	1.0	1.0

Source: Bureau of Census and Statistics, *Philippines Census of Population and Housing*, 1970.

Table 3.3: Distribution of Education by Occupation in Sri Lanka, 1963 and 1971

Occupations	Proportion of labour force		Average no. of years of education		Proportion of total number of years of education		Distribution of educational investment units		(5)/(1)	(6)/(2)	(7)/(1)	(8)/(2)
	1963 (1)	1971 (2)	1963 (3)	1971 (4)	1963 (5)	1971 (6)	1963 (7)	1971 (8)	(9)	(10)	(11)	(12)
Professional and managerial	5.6	5.3	11.0	12.3	12.9	12.0	18.3	17.4	2.2	2.1	3.1	3.1
Clerical	3.8	4.0	9.7	10.6	7.6	7.6	9.6	9.9	1.9	1.8	2.4	2.4
Sales	6.7	7.8	6.1	7.0	8.5	10.0	8.8	10.2	1.2	1.2	1.3	1.3
Agriculture	52.8	50.7	3.5	3.6	38.4	33.5	32.4	26.4	0.7	0.6	0.6	0.5
Production	22.8	26.6	5.1	6.5	24.2	31.7	23.2	31.3	1.0	1.1	1.0	1.1
Services	8.2	5.5	4.8	5.2	8.3	5.3	7.7	4.8	1.0	0.9	0.9	0.8
All	100.0	100.0	4.8	5.4	100.0	100.0	100.0	100.0	1.0	1.0	1.0	1.0

Source: Department of Census and Statistics, *Ceylon/Sri Lanka Census of Population*, 1963 and 1971.

Educational Expansion and the Labour Market 43

keep up a high proportion of the years of education available, it is interesting to speculate on when the thirst for more years of education in those occupations will be satisfied. One clue to this is the relation of education to occupation in more highly educated and less education-scarce nations. Table 3.4 compares Sri Lanka, the Philippines and Hong Kong to the USA. By and large, average educational levels in occupational groups in those three Asian countries are considerably below US levels, although the gap did close slightly in the 1960s. The gap was smallest in white-collar occupations — professional, managerial and clerical; it was larger in sales and production, and greatest in agriculture. Of course, there is nothing sacrosanct about US educational levels. There must, however, be a suspicion that certainly for white-collar occupations in the near future, and for sales and production workers in the next twenty or thirty years, more movement towards US levels can be expected.

Table 3.4 is very depressing in that way: in 1969 in the USA professional workers had on average 70 per cent more years of education than agricultural workers; in the Philippines and Sri Lanka the gap was over 200 per cent. If, in order to reduce the gap in years of education between agricultural and professional workers to US dimensions, it is first necessary to go through a process of raising the years of education of all other occupations to double figures, the process can be expected to take over a century.

Age and the Labour Market

A factor not mentioned so far is age. It was shown in the previous chapter that age interacts with educational level, and does so differently for different occupations. Significant shifts in the age pattern of the labour force can thus be expected to have their own effect on income distribution. Data on age exist only for Sri Lanka and are given in Table 3.5. It is interesting that the labour force in general grew hardly older during the intercensal period, from 34.7 to 34.8 years of age. However, the unemployed grew a lot younger and increased considerably in numbers, while the employed grew, on average, nearly one year older.[1] If we look at the data by occupational group, the big jump in the service occupations is hard to believe; otherwise all the changes were slight. However, the service sector definitely registered a shift from lower-level services (mainly household and domestic work) to higher-level including protective services (i.e. police etc.) during the

Table 3.4: Education Levels by Occupation in Selected Countries, in Terms of Number of Years of Education

Occupations	USA: *median* and average number of years of education				Percentages in relation to the USA (averages)				
					Sri Lanka		Philippines		Hong Kong
	1959		1969		c. 1960	c. 1970	c. 1960	c. 1970	c. 1970
Professional	*16.2*	17.2	*16.3*	17.3	n.a.	n.a.	82	82	70
Managerial	*12.4*	14.3	*12.7*	14.6	n.a.	n.a.	69	70	60
Professional and managerial	*13.5*	14.6	*14.9*	16.1	75	76	79	80	66
Clerical	*12.5*	13.3	*12.6*	13.4	73	79	94	97)	
Sales	*12.4*	14.1	*12.6*	14.3	43	49	49	52)	62 (app.)
Agriculture	*8.6*	9.3	*9.3*	10.1	38	36	46	46	26
Services	*9.7*	9.5	*11.3*	11.1	50	47	71	62	52
Production	*10.0*	12.0	*11.4*	13.7	42	47	57	52	47
All	*12.0*	12.3	*12.4*	12.7	39	42	49	51	55

Sources: For USA, median figures are given in *Handbook of Labour Statistics, 1970*. Averages for 1969 were calculated from US Department of Commerce, Bureau of the Census, *Earnings by Occupation and Education*, 1973. The same ratio of median to average years of education was assumed to apply in 1959. Other countries — national censuses.

period. In general, persons in professional and clerical occupations grew marginally older, which is consistent with the insistence on higher educational standards for recruitment and with the enlistment of fewer young workers. Production and sales workers, whose share of the labour force expanded, grew younger.

Table 3.5: Mean Age by Occupation and Employment Status in Sri Lanka, 1963 and 1971

Occupation or employment status	1963	1971
Professional etc.	36.4	36.9
Clerical	34.5	34.7
Sales	36.1	35.8
Service	32.0	38.8
Agriculture	36.1	36.0
Production	34.7	34.2
All employed	35.4	36.3
Unemployed*	26.2	23.8

*Actively seeking work only.
Source: Department of Census and Statistics, *Census of Population*, 1963 and 1971.

The Distribution of Education and Income

Gini coefficients can also be given for Sri Lanka and the Philippines for years of education by occupation and, although for the Philippines hardly satisfactorily, for main occupation incomes. Table 3.6 gives the data. The general trend in both countries was towards a reduction in the spread of years of education, helped naturally by a sharp reduction in the proportion of workers with no education at all. In Sri Lanka all occupations except in services witnessed a noticeable decrease in their Gini coefficients for the distribution of years of education. In the Philippines the reduction was generally less, and, for example, was absent for production workers. Nor is the pattern between the two countries very consistent, although agriculture has the greatest spread in both and clerical and professional workers the least. It can be noted that for the distribution of years of education in all professional, administrative and clerical occupations US data yield Gini coefficients of around 0.10. Therefore the distribution of education in those occupations in Sri Lanka may not change much in the future, although the educational inflation, i.e. increase in the average number of years of education, may well continue. In the Philippines there is already a greater polarisation of educational levels in professional occupations than in the USA.

Table 3.6: Gini Coefficients for Years of Education and Main Occupation Incomes in the Philippines and Sri Lanka

Occupations	Philippines				Sri Lanka			
	Years of education		Incomes*		Years of education		Incomes	
	c. 1960	c. 1970	1965	1971	1963	1971	1963	1973
Professional	0.06	0.05	0.42	0.35)	0.17	0.12	0.33	0.30
Administrative	0.25	0.23	0.50	0.38)				
Clerical	0.10	0.09	0.39	0.32	0.18	0.11	0.34	0.26
Sales	0.31	0.29	0.48	0.46	0.25	0.22	0.52	0.40
Agriculture	0.42	0.38	0.42	0.43	0.49	0.46	0.44	0.30
Production	0.27	0.27	0.36	0.34	0.31	0.20	0.34	0.34
Services	0.35	0.26	0.34	0.39	0.39	0.39	0.38	0.39
All employed	0.39	0.36	0.51	0.49	0.43	0.39	0.47	0.39

*Income of a household headed by a member with that occupation.
Sources: National census and, for the Philippines, family income and expenditure surveys; for Sri Lanka, consumer finance surveys.

For the Philippines the Gini coefficients for the distribution of income are for the household incomes of households headed by a member of an occupational group.[2] The Sri Lanka data are for main occupation incomes, although income generated by unpaid family workers is chalked up to the head of the household. In general, the coefficients for the Philippines are higher, probably indicating a greater degree of inequality in distribution, although between occupations the pattern is not so very different. For services and production workers in the early 1970s the coefficient is identical. In Sri Lanka, services and sales are least equal and clerical occupations most equal. Surprisingly, agriculture has by no means the most unequal distribution, which is in both cases reserved for sales. In the Philippines the distribution is still the most equal in clerical occupations, with sales and agriculture the least equal. However, between the dates given there have been considerable changes in the order. In 1965, administrative workers were the most unequal in the Philippines and services the least. In the six intervening years administrative earnings became much more equal (because of underreporting at the top?) and earnings in services much more unequal. The same thing apparently happened to a minor degree in Sri Lanka. In 1963 in Sri Lanka, the distribution of incomes was most unequal for sales workers and least unequal for professional workers.

Educational Expansion and the Labour Market

However, income distribution among white-collar workers has consistently narrowed, with the spread of incomes among clerical workers falling in both countries.

In Sri Lanka it is possible to distinguish two major groups of occupations, those where the distribution of income improved faster than the improvement in the distribution of education, and those where the opposite took place. The latter group, where the equalisation of education proceeded more quickly than that of incomes, includes professional, clerical and production workers, largely wage earners. For the self-employed, mainly in agriculture and sales, incomes moved towards equality more quickly than did education levels. Human capital may well have been neglected by comparison with other forms of capital. The Philippines between 1965 and 1971 presents no such clear picture. In most occupations equalisation proceeded more quickly for education than for income.

Incomes by Education

Further information for Sri Lanka and the Philippines can be given on incomes by educational group. Table 3.7 gives Gini coefficients for main occupation incomes by educational level for Sri Lanka (1963 and 1973) and coefficients for household incomes for the Philippines (1971) are given in Table 3.8. The tables also take into account unemployment by education group and give Gini coefficients by education level taking the unemployed as zero income receivers. Generally, but with the exceptions primarily of college graduates, the Gini coefficients for the employed are lower in Sri Lanka, and if the unemployed are also taken into account the figures for workers with no schooling remain lower in Sri Lanka. That country's experience between 1963 and 1973 was of a general reduction in the inequality of main occupation incomes by education. The reduction was largest for the illiterate, which is not surprising since the supply of young and low-paid workers to that sector has been sharply reduced. In the more highly educated sectors unemployment rose considerably, keeping a number of younger workers out of the employed labour force. Gini coefficients including unemployment show only very slight falls in the more highly educated groups.

It is also interesting to compare Gini coefficients for the distribution of income by education level with those by occupation given in Table 3.6. In Sri Lanka the latter are generally lower than the former, i.e. there is greater equality in the distribution of incomes by occupation than by education level (in such cases, for example, as those of professional and clerical workers having completed their secondary education and those above that level, or production workers with primary and secondary education). This feature becomes even more marked when account is taken of educated unemployment. In the Philippines, for similar groups, we find the pattern to be the same, especially if we compare the income distribution of people having received only an elementary education with the income distribution of production and service workers.

Table 3.7: Gini Coefficients of Main Occupation Incomes by Level of Education in Sri Lanka, 1963-73

	Gini coefficients				Unemployment rate (%)**	
	For the employed only		Including the unemployed*			
Level of education	1963	1973	1963	1973	1963	1971
No schooling, illiterate	0.45	0.35	0.47	0.38)	4.0	4.6
No schooling, literate	0.41	0.36	0.43	0.39)		
Primary	0.40	0.37	0.44	0.39	6.1	3.0
Secondary	0.44	0.37	0.54	0.51	16.8	22.0
School leaving certificate, ordinary level	0.42	0.34	0.56	0.55	23.5	32.1
Above	0.46	0.40	0.48	0.47	2.8	12.8

*Taking incomes of the unemployed as zero.
**These unemployment rates apply as much to rural as to urban areas.
Source: Central Bank of Ceylon consumer finance surveys, and national censuses.

It is interesting also to see how average incomes by educational level changed over the period. As Table 3.9 shows, in Sri Lanka, the spread of incomes between the two extremes of the educational ladder narrowed very considerably.[3] In fact there is a great change in rates of increase by education level between the primary and the secondary level. This change corresponds to the pattern of unemployment by education level. When account is taken of the unemployed as zero income receivers, rates of increase of incomes of the more highly educated fall, relatively, even further. Age, of course, is a factor strengthening the pattern of higher increases for the less educated. Data for the spread of incomes can also be given for the Philippines (Table 3.10); these in fact show less spread than the Sri Lanka data, whether adjusted for unemployment or not.

Table 3.8: Gini Coefficients of Household Income by Level of Education of the Household Head in the Philippines, 1971

Level of education	Gini coefficients		Unemployment rate (%)
	For the employed only	Including the unemployed	
No schooling	0.47	0.49	*4.4*
Elementary 1-3	0.44	0.46	*4.5*
Elementary 4+	0.55	0.58	*6.8*
High school 1-2	0.35	0.44	*13.7*
High school 3-4	0.41	0.50	*15.3*
College	0.35	0.43	*12.2*

Source: Bureau of Census and Statistics, *Family Incomes and Expenditures*, 1971.

Incomes by Occupation

While the spread of income by education level is much less in the Philippines than in Sri Lanka, comparable data on the spread of wages and salaries by occupation in the two countries show the Philippines to have the greater differences (see Table 3.11). Furthermore, during the 1960s there would appear to have been a widening of interoccupational wage and salary differentials in the Philippines not only in relation to the wages of agricultural workers but also within urban areas. Sri Lanka, on the other hand, experienced an overall narrowing of differentials in relation to the salaries of professional workers. In both countries, however, the gap between urban and clerical workers on the one hand and agricultural workers on the other increased; and in both countries clerical workers, despite the concentration of unemployment in the educational groups which supply clerical workers, improved their position in relation to professional workers.[4] The data for these two countries can be contrasted with those for the USA between 1959 and 1969. There, by contrast, all differentials narrowed in relation to agricultural workers. However, in that country the incomes of clerical workers fell in relation to those of both professional workers and urban labour.

One point of interest is the relation of teachers' incomes to others. This is relevant to the overall social cost of the educational system, since the lower the relative income of the teaching profession the higher will be average rates of return to education and the cheaper the achievement of higher levels of education. Table 3.11 shows that by the end of the 1960s the ratio of secondary school teachers' earnings to agricultural workers' earnings was 4.6:1 in Sri Lanka and 3.7:1 in the

Table 3.9: Variations in Mean Incomes by Educational Level in Sri Lanka, 1963-73 (in rupees and percentage index numbers)

Level of education	Excluding the unemployed			Including the unemployed*		
	1963	1973	Rise (%) 1963-73	1963	1973	Rise (%) 1963-73
No schooling, illiterate	129 (100)	255 (100)	98	124 (100)	243 (100)	96
No schooling, literate	211 (163)	362 (142)	72	203 (164)	345 (142)	70
Primary	225 (174)	411 (161)	83	211 (170)	399 (164)	89
Secondary	366 (284)	539 (211)	47	304 (245)	420 (173)	38
School leaving certificate, ordinary level	600 (465)	742 (291)	24	459 (370)	504 (207)	10
Above	1,040 (806)	1,411 (553)	36	1,011 (815)	1,237 (509)	22
Average	207	299	44			

*Taking unemployed as zero income receivers.
Source: As for Table 3.7.

Educational Expansion and the Labour Market

Table 3.10: Family Income by Education of Household Head in the Philippines, 1971 (in pesos and percentage index numbers)

		Percentage index numbers	
Level of education	Pesos	Employed only	Including unemployed*
No schooling	2,264	(100)	(100)
Elementary 1-3	2,411	(106)	(106)
Elementary 4+	3,000	(132)	(129)
High school 1-2	3,053	(135)	(122)
High school 3-4	4,536	(201)	(178)
College	7,755	(342)	(315)

*Taking the unemployed as zero income receivers.
Source: As for Table 3.8.

Table 3.11: Relative Wage and Salary Levels in the Philippines, Sri Lanka and the USA (agricultural labour = 1.0)

Occupations	Philippines		Sri Lanka		USA	
	1960	1971	1963	1973	1959	1969
Professional	3.5	4.3	4.2	4.1	5.2	3.1
Clerical	2.4	3.5	3.4	3.8	3.4	1.8
Urban labour	1.7	2.3	1.4	1.9	2.7	1.8
Large-scale industries	2.6	3.5	n.a.	2.1	n.a.	n.a.
Secondary teacher	3.1	3.7	5.2	4.6	4.8	2.7
Primary teacher	3.3	4.2	3.6	3.7	3.9	2.3
Ratios						
Prof.: Clerical	*1.5*	*1.1*	*1.2*	*1.1*	*1.5*	*1.7*
Prof.: Urb. labour	*2.0*	*2.0*	*3.0*	*2.2*	*1.9*	*1.7*
Sec.T.:Urb. labour	*1.8*	*1.6*	*3.7*	*2.5*	*1.8*	*1.5*
Prim.T.: Urb. labour	*1.9*	*1.8*	*2.5*	*2.0*	*2.7*	*1.8*

Sources: Philippines, Wage and Position Classification Office, Bureau of Agricultural Economics, and government pay scales; Sri Lanka, consumer finance surveys; USA, national census.

Philippines but only 2.7:1 in the USA. The US ratio is compatible with a large education sector, and hence a high proportion of secondary school teachers in the labour force, and a small agricultural sector.

The Effect of Educated Unemployment

Both the Philippines and Sri Lanka had rates of educated unemployment in double figures at the end of the 1960s and in the early 1970s.

52 *Educational Expansion and the Labour Market*

In both countries the government is a major employer: in the Philippines some 70 per cent of professional, 60 per cent of managerial and 50 per cent of clerical workers are in government employment. Exact data for Sri Lanka are not available, but with virtually no private education services and very little private practice of Western medicine the proportion will no doubt be greater. In both countries the government is the major employer of persons with over 8-10 years of education.

The job competition approach which we discussed in the previous chapter predicts that a surplus of educated job-seekers results in a downward shift in their average occupation. Data for Sri Lanka, in Table 3.12, show that this shift has been very slow.

For the Philippines (Table 3.13) the shift would appear to have been greater, not perhaps for the college-educated, but for those at the next level. However, these data are compatible with a consolidation of the position of college-educated people within occupations. In the Philippines the proportion of male college graduates in professional, managerial and clerical occupations respectively rose from 57 per cent to 79 per cent, 12 to 35 per cent and 27 to 35 per cent. In Sri Lanka the respective changes were rises from 8 to 24 per cent, and from 6 to 17 per cent, and a fall from 5 to 2 per cent. Generally, therefore, the more highly educated are increasing their hold on the higher-status occupations, so that some predictions of the job competition model are verified.

Table 3.12: Occupational Breakdown of Persons at Selected Educational Levels in Sri Lanka

Occupations	Males				Females			
	1963		1971		1963		1971	
	OL	D	OL	D	OL	D	OL	D
Prof. etc.	29.5	69.0	28.7	65.6	80.2	92.9	72.2	71.1
Admin. etc.	4.7	17.3	1.9	8.2	0.5	2.2	0.3	1.4
Clerical	30.7	5.5	32.9	17.7	7.8	1.9	12.3	25.1
Other	35.1	8.2	36.5	8.5	11.5	3.0	15.2	2.4
All	100.0	100.0	100.0	100.0	100.0	100.0	100.0	100.0

Key: D = Degree+; OL = ordinary level plus higher school certificate or advanced level.
Source: *Census of Population.*

Table 3.13: Occupational Breakdown of Persons at Selected Educational Levels in the Philippines

	Males				Females			
Occupations	1961		1970		1961		1970	
	HS	C	HS	C	HS	C	HS	C
Prof. etc.	7.8	39.8	4.1	50.4	24.1	68.7	12.6	74.6
Admin. etc.	6.9	9.4	2.9	7.7	7.6	3.5	1.9	1.4
Clerical	15.9	27.7	11.8	18.7	14.3	18.3	19.1	16.4
Other	69.4	23.1	81.2	23.2	54.0	9.5	66.4	7.6
All	100.0	100.0	100.0	100.0	100.0	100.0	100.0	100.0

Key: HS (1961) = high school 4 years + college 1-3 years;
HS (1970) = high school completed and college started;
C (1961) = college 4 years + ; C (1970) = college completed.
Sources: April 1961 labour force survey; 1970 census.

Further, in accordance with the job competition model, people with a secondary education in Sri Lanka experienced a lower rate of income increase than did graduates.[5] However, it must also be pointed out that both groups had lower rates of increase than all other (lower) educational groups. Furthermore, the relative rates of increase of earnings of the various educational groups very nearly follow the ordering of their rates of unemployment, which would be a point in favour of a wage competition approach. In fact, of course, wage competition also takes place by the very fact that there are people who remain without jobs and hence without incomes. Private lifetime incomes are lowered by late starts in permanent employment. The fact that competition of this kind in fact brings no benefits to the employer may not be unrelated to the fact that for most of the educated the employer is the government. Wage flexibility is lost by the existence of one major employer.

In Sri Lanka and the Philippines as much as anywhere else, government wage systems are apt to be inflexible. Under such systems it is difficult formally to re-rank occupations, although some action can, of course, be taken to speed up or retard promotions or expansion. During the 1960s and early 1970s government salaries lagged on the average in both Sri Lanka and the Philippines. At first they were proportionally higher in Sri Lanka than in the Philippines, but over the period the trend in the two countries was similar. In addition there was some levelling in the government pay structures of both countries, with rates for unskilled workers rising faster than for professionals.

54 *Educational Expansion and the Labour Market*

There is indeed some evidence, for professional workers in the Philippines and for clerical workers in Sri Lanka, that rates of pay may have been rising faster in the private sector than in the public sector. For Sri Lanka the data are not convincing because the trend of average earnings for clerical workers in government is not known. They may have risen much faster than did pay scales.

While government pay scales cannot be very flexible, their designers display no great eagerness to make them so. A Cabinet subcommittee in Sri Lanka reported on pay scales in public corporations; the data refer to 1971. It found that average earnings for clerical workers ranged from Rs 330 to 350, while pay for skilled craftsmen was about Rs 240. The report recommended that most clerical workers should continue to be paid more than most skilled manual workers but that the latter should have increased promotion possibilities, with a possible maximum wage above the maximum for clerical workers. In the same year, average earnings for clerical workers in the retail trade amounted to Rs 200. It is quite likely that the existence of even a slight chance of government employment strengthens job-seekers' resolve not to accept lower-paid jobs in the private sector, so that the existence of unemployment is consistent with rising wages outside government employment.

Limited Income Effects of Education as Such

First, the detailed evidence from the Philippines and Sri Lanka in this chapter suggests a tendency for educational levels as between certain countries, measured in years, to approximate where levels of technology approximate. Educational levels of clerical and professional workers can probably be expected to converge long before the educational levels of agricultural and other workers. Physicians and engineers have identical levels of education, whereas casual workers do not. If this tendency indeed prevailed generally it would follow that attempts to spread years of education more equally throughout any labour force would appear to be doomed until higher, wealthier or more influential occupational groups had satisfied their educational aspirations. Hence perhaps the very slight changes in the distribution of educational investment, as measured by Gini coefficients, in the labour forces of the Philippines and Sri Lanka during the 1960s. In higher occupational groups, predominantly white-collar workers, the spread of educational levels can be expected to narrow, thus effectively making entry more difficult for the less educated. Access to good education and persistence in education through college are of crucial importance in determining income.

However, it is also fairly clear that the length of the education of any group is not a good predictor, particularly when national income is stagnant. It can, for example, be mentioned that throughout the 1960s the real incomes of nearly all white-collar groups fell in both Sri Lanka and the Philippines. Thus investment in human capital did not always give a good return on average, although the marginal rates of return to different levels of education have often been high and positive. Of course, to a much more pronounced extent than Western countries, countries in Asia are not meritocracies; or rather, the sector where intellectual merit alone is important in determining income levels is small and largely under a monopoly employer. Throughout the agricultural sector, most of the commercial sector and the informal sector, access to physical capital is the predominant consideration and concern. This is not to deny that the actors in these economic sectors will not make better decisions and higher profits with more education; probably they will.

There may be objections to calling the modern sectors of most Asian economies meritocratic. It so often turns out that the higher posts are after all taken primarily by people with a good social background, because, for example, the qualifications required may include fluency in a Western language. To some extent also, governments set their pay scales to support unnecessary educational distinctions – for example paying more for more highly educated school teachers. Moreover, there is no guarantee that length of unemployment and job search are inversely related to merit.

A tentative conclusion of this chapter must be that the distribution of work incomes, at least in the countries we have studied in depth, owes much more to the distribution of occupations, and to factors[6] operating on occupational incomes independently of educational level, than to the distribution of education. With regard to the agricultural labour force, for example, in the Philippines the number of years of education received rose faster than the average, but the level of income declined in relation to that in other occupations; in Sri Lanka, on the other hand, the exact opposite occurred. In the Sri Lanka labour force in general, income increases were related more or less inversely to education level. Although the educational level became considerably more uniform for the highest occupational group, it could not hold its relative income line against clerical and urban labour groups. Obviously, government pay policy, which in both Sri Lanka and the Philippines was egalitarian within its own subsystem, played a part in this development. However, the operation of government pay policies also demonstrates the limits of wage competition. In both countries the position of clerical workers was apparently strengthened in relation to both the higher-level occupations and to agricultural workers, despite educated unemployment.

Notes

1. It is interesting to note that the share of female workers increased in the occupations of professional and technical workers, agriculture and production work. Furthermore, female workers are, on average, younger than male. This may account for the fall in the average age of agricultural and production workers. Among professional workers the spread in years of age must have widened.

2. This itself is most likely to increase the value of the coefficients. Furthermore, in the Philippines women predominate in the professional workers category, but they may not be heads of households.

3. It is interesting to note that while the proportion of girls increased among workers who had obtained their school leaving certificate, it fell in the category of workers having reached a higher educational level. The reduction in the spread of earnings by education group is therefore not, or not solely, the result of any changing sex composition.

4. This change may be partly due to the relatively small proportion of female workers in clerical occupations, by comparison with the usually very large proportion of female workers in the professions, including teaching. However, the relative position of the latter group varied greatly between the two countries.

5. We have already noted that the proportion of female workers rose among workers with a secondary education and fell in the more highly educated group.

6. One of which could be the sex composition of an occupation.

4 INTERNATIONAL COMPARISONS I (GENERAL PATTERN OF INEQUALITY)

This chapter attempts to show the general pattern of inequality in education by comparing the achievement test scores of schoolchildren from poor countries with those of schoolchildren of comparable age or grade from rich countries. The comparisons we have made at this stage are broad ones as a starting point for a detailed analysis of the situation in particular countries which is carried out in the next two chapters.

The scores of the test used in the analysis are those in reading skill.[1] Reading is universally regarded as a requisite not only for gathering information but also for processing it: as a skill, reading comprehension shows how people decode symbols from a printed page; it can also reveal the extent of the reader's mental grasp, and from that something can be inferred about the reader's mental life.

Our analysis[2] adds something to what is generally known. Besides re-emphasising what the authors on whom we draw have already shown, i.e. that the reading comprehension skill of children from less developed countries is very much inferior to that of children from more advanced countries,[3] Table 4.1 adds a new twist: that the differences in reading skill are much greater in the older samples of schoolchildren. This suggests that initial gaps in reading skill widen towards the later years of schooling, despite the fact that at that stage the schoolchildren in less developed countries are the cream of their school age population.

As to the pattern of skills in reading comprehension, the differences are again sharply prominent. At the complex levels (see Table 4.2, items B and E), the gaps are extremely wide. Only in simple reading skill do the test responses differ narrowly.

Causal factors relating to test scores in reading affect not only the average scores but also their spread or their frequency distribution.[4] We describe this distribution by the coefficient of variation, which is obtained by dividing the standard deviation by its corresponding mean. We multiply this quotient by 100 to express it in percentage terms. A small coefficient means that the scores are closely clustered around the average; it also means a low spread or low inequality in the reading scores. A large one means the opposite. Our calculations show that the coefficients of variation from the three less developed countries vary

Table 4.1: Results of Reading Comprehension Tests in Selected Advanced and Less Developed Countries (averages in standard units: u = o)

Countries*	Pop. I	Pop. II	Pop. IV
Less developed countries	− 12.33	− 17.00	− 23.67
Advanced countries	0.27	0.92	3.17
Difference	*− 12.60***	*− 17.92***	*− 26.84***

*See note 1 to this chapter.
**Significant at 1 per cent P (probability) level.
Key: I = Ten-year-olds; II = Fourteen-year-olds; IV = Pupils in their final year of pre-university education, regardless of age.
Source: Calculations from David A. Walker, *The IEA Six-Subject Survey — An Empirical Study of Education in Twenty-One Countries*, International Studies in Evaluation IX (Stockholm, Almquist and Wiksell, 1975), Table 6.4, p. 114.

Table 4.2: Average Percentage of Pupils Passing Reading Comprehension Tests in Selected Advanced and Less Developed Countries, Ten-year-olds (Chile, India and Iran)

Item	Advanced countries	Less developed countries	Difference
A. Word or phrase in context	89.73	70.67	19.06*
B. Identifying antecedents or references	63.55	37.00	26.55*
C. Answering questions from answers given in passage	55.45	41.33	14.12
D. Drawing inferences from passage	67.27	49.67	17.60*
E. Determining writer's purpose, point of view	61.64	37.67	23.97*

*Significant at 1 per cent P level.
Source: Calculations from Walker, *IEA Survey*, Table 6.5, p. 116. Walker's results were presented in a somewhat negative way, i.e. in percentage failure. Without loss of information, we transformed them into percentage passing.

widely (see Table 4.3). Chile, for instance, seems to show test results that are less and less spread as one moves from Population I (ten-year-olds) to Population II (fourteen-year-olds) and on to Population IV (pupils in their final year of pre-university education, regardless of age). India, however, exhibits an opposite trend, and Iran is somewhere in between. These observations are quite different from those that can be made on the basis of the figures from the advanced countries. The decrease in the size of the coefficient is much more sharp in those

International Comparisons I 59

countries than in the less developed. Hence, the progress in the levelling up of reading ability appears to be much faster in the advanced countries than that in the three that are less developed.

Table 4.3: Coefficient of Variation of Total Scores for Reading Comprehension in Selected Less Developed and Advanced Countries

Country	Pop. I	Pop. II	Pop. IV
Chile	102.20	78.72	55.00
India	110.59	138.46	165.71
Iran	186.49	85.90	136.36
Average	*133.09*	*101.03*	*119.02*
Average for advanced countries	*58.97*	*41.06*	*33.76*

Source: Calculated from Robert L. Thorndike, *Reading Comprehension in Fifteen Countries* (Stockholm, Almquist and Wiksell, 1973), Tables 8.1, 8.2 and 8.3, pp. 124ff.

From the analysis of the coefficients of variation of total scores, we now turn to those of the subscores, especially to those of subtest E. This subtest evaluates a complex reading skill, namely the reader's 'ability to determine the purpose, intent and point of view of the writer'.[5] The coefficients in Table 4.4 give the impression that in the advanced countries the scores are increasingly clustered around the mean as the pupils progress toward the upper levels of schooling. In the less developed countries, however, the trend tends to be the opposite: the scores appear dispersed unevenly or unequally, and most probably very thinly. This observation is consistent with what was said earlier, and it gives us a better picture of the level and distribution of reading ability of schoolchildren from two different parts of the world.[6]

By comparing and contrasting the test scores of schoolchildren from the less developed countries and of those from the advanced countries, we have thus found the following:

(a) There are large differences in achievement test scores between schoolchildren from less developed countries and those of advanced countries.
(b) The increments in average scores from one age group to another seem to indicate that the levelling up of reading ability among schoolchildren from the advanced countries is fast while that of the schoolchildren from the three less developed countries is quite slow.
(c) As a consequence of this point ((b) above), the gaps tend to widen

Table 4.4: Differences in Average of Means and of Coefficient of Variation Relation to Subscore E (Ability to Determine the Writer's Purpose, Intent and Point of View) in Selected Advanced and Less Developed Countries

Item	Pop. I	Pop. II	Pop. IV
Average of means			
Advanced countries	1.76	2.43	3.08
Less developed countries	0.47	1.00	1.00
Difference	1.29*	1.43*	2.08*
Average coefficient of variation			
Advanced countries	132.41	72.62	54.13
Less developed countries	189.21	178.59	326.35
Difference	−56.80*	−105.97*	−272.22*

*Significant at 1 per cent P level.
Source: Calculated from Thorndike, *Reading Comprehension*, Tables 8.1, 8.2 and 8.3, pp. 124ff.

with time spent in school. Small initial gaps become very large much later.
(d) Low average scores of schoolchildren from the less developed countries are matched by an uneven distribution.

Notes

1. Many of the results reported in this chapter are the outcome of secondary analysis of data from an international survey conducted by the International Association for the Evaluation of Educational Achievement (IEA). Among the countries that participated, Chile, India, Iran and Thailand were classified as less developed, whereas the others (Australia, Belgium, Finland, France, the Federal Republic of Germany, Hungary, Ireland, Sweden, the United Kingdom and the United States) were classified as advanced.

Samples of schoolchildren were chosen and tested in science, reading comprehension, literature, French, English and civics. For a variety of reasons, schoolchildren from some countries were not able to participate in all the subjects. Thai children, for example, were not in the reading test, and children from many countries were not tested in French. The reliability coefficients of the reading test are moderately high both in the less developed and in the advanced countries, so that a clear comparison of the reading skills of schoolchildren from these groups of countries can be made. The reading comprehension test was designed in such a way that it could be used across languages in all of the different participating countries, and be of comparable difficulty in each language (into which it was translated). (Robert L. Thorndike, *Reading Comprehension in Fifteen Countries* (Stockholm, Almquist and Wiksell, 1973), p. 30.)

2. Based on data drawn from Thorndike and from David A. Walker, *The IEA Six-Subject Survey − An Empirical Study of Education in Twenty-One Countries*, International Studies in Evaluation IX (Stockholm, Almquist and

Wiksell, 1975).

3. According to Thorndike, *Reading Comprehension*, p. 177, 'the differences are so large that by the standards of the developed countries, the 14-year olds in the developing countries seem almost illiterate'.

4. Byron W. Brown and Daniel H. Saks, 'The Production and Distribution of Cognitive Skills Within Schools', *Journal of Political Economy*, Vol. 83 (June 1975), p. 571.

5. Thorndike, *Reading Comprehension*, p. 56.

6. It must be borne in mind, however, that differences in scores, including their variability, are partly due to the test itself, i.e. its discriminating power at low levels of ability. Hence a need for caution in the interpretation of those differences.

5 INTERNATIONAL COMPARISONS II (THINKING ABILITY OF CHILDREN OF LABOURERS AND OF EXECUTIVES AND PROFESSIONALS)

In the preceding chapter, scholastic achievement was studied in a general way. Test scores of children from poor countries were found to be much lower than those of children from rich countries. To our mind this finding implies an association between low scholastic achievement and deprived conditions. Such an association could perhaps explain variations in the achievement of schoolchildren within individual less developed countries. These observations seem to confirm general impressions, and they may not be surprising to many readers. However, from an egalitarian point of view, the magnitude of the variations or differences is quite disturbing.

In the present chapter[1] scholastic achievement is studied further, in such a way as to bring into sharp focus the structure of the differences in thinking ability,[2] which has been seen on the frontier of research as fundamental in generating inequality in the wide sense.[3] The main concern of this chapter is to demonstrate that wide qualitative differences in scholastic achievement exist in spite of more or less equal ages or years of schooling. This demonstration is accomplished by analysing the different levels of thinking ability[4] as revealed by the test responses of children whose fathers are at different levels of the occupational hierarchy. The result of this analysis further shows why equalising years of schooling, as orthodox policies seem to advocate, would have hardly any desirable impact (a) on patterns of skill distribution and (b), as a long-term effect, on income distribution.

Implicitly we assess equality in terms of abilities created. The reason is that this is what schooling and training are all about: they create abilities, whether for the purpose of work or of leisure. In this instance we have chosen thinking ability since it is important for survival in the modern world. At work, this is the quality that is often most scarce: there is usually a much higher premium on it than on other forms of ability. This being so, distributing ability (via the learning process) is obviously much better than distributing certificates: there is a fair chance that ability will have more effect than certificates on the desirable changes of future income distribution.

International Comparisons II 63

In this chapter we put forward the view that there is a causal link between the occupations of parents and the scholastic achievements of their children. This view is supported by (a) statistically significant association between the two variables, and (b) their sequence of occurrence, i.e. the supposed cause (occupation of parents) precedes the supposed effect (achievement of children). Admittedly achievement can also be influenced by other factors. It is even plausible that parents' occupation as such has no direct effect on children's scholastic achievement: instead, occupation may operate through many mediating (or intervening) factors. This linkage would be demonstrable (or falsifiable) by introducing a third variable which would render the association between the first two trivial. If such variable is found, then that same variable may be said to mediate the effect of occupation on achievement. This framework is illustrated, for example, by the sequence: occupation (or employment) → income → household environment and other factors → achievement. Here, income, household environment and other factors are supposed to mediate the effect of parental occupation on children's scholastic achievement. Short of making rigorous inferences on causality, it is sufficient for us to show that there exist wide differences in the scholastic achievement of children whose fathers' occupations are different.

Representativity of Samples

This work focuses on Asian countries, but data constraints limit us in this chapter to India, Iran and Thailand, the Asian countries which participated in the IEA survey.

The schoolchildren included in the analysis are those designated by the IEA as Populatien II and Population IV; these are fourteen-year-olds and pupils in the final year of their pre-tertiary education (regardless of age), respectively. Fourteen-year-old children can be in different grade levels: the middle two-thirds of the sample are from grades 6 to 9 in India, 7 to 8 in Iran and 8 to 9 in Thailand. In Population IV it is the age that varies rather than the grade. Since countries do not have the same school system, and since the number of curriculum years to reach the final year of pre-tertiary studies varies from one country to another, the ages of the pupils in this population tend to be different. This observation is supported by the following age averages of the samples: about 17 in India, 18 in Thailand and 19 in Iran.

It is also worth mentioning some significant and necessary exclusions from the sampling of the target population. Peaker states that, in general, 'the specified populations were sampled in all the participating countries'. However, there were problems in India and in Thailand. The Indian data were gathered from six Hindi-speaking states, and did not include English-medium private schools; children who were 14 years old but who could not read nor write were for obvious reasons excluded from the testing exercise. In Thailand, 14 out of 71 provinces could not be reached at the time of the survey for security reasons; therefore, the findings and interpretations drawn from the data would not necessarily apply to the excluded provinces.[5]

This background information on the samples should be a sufficient reason for showing caution in interpreting the data, and for avoiding inter-country comparisons concerning the level of test performance.

Occupational Categories

Home background has been known to affect the scholastic achievement of children and we shall see that in the countries examined in this chapter, differences in scholastic achievement are associated with variations in home background.

As a variable, home background can be measured or represented in many ways. For example, it can be indicated by the income level of households. This measure reflects the stream of goods and services that are consumed by the household of which the pupil is a member. The same variable can also be measured by what sociologists call 'socio-economic status'. This represents the position of the household in the social structure; it describes lifestyles, and connotes exposure to various kinds of socialising experiences. Another way of representing home background is by means of the occupation of parents. This indicator reveals not only income levels but also socio-economic status.

In societies or economies which are characterised by highly specialised division of labour, occupations are stratified into classes. On the average, occupational categories have different, stratifiable income levels; in the same fashion, people in different occupations have widely different lifestyles, which create different learning environments in their homes.

Among the indicators of home background, we find that the use of occupational categories is most convenient. First, the concept is relatively simple; it is readily understood by a wide audience. Secondly, it is closely linked to real people whose identity is easily seen: the problems of those people and the policy needed to help them are quickly grasped even by the least sophisticated. And finally, our choice of this variable was influenced by data availability.

The IEA data include information on the occupations of the fathers, which are classified into nine categories ranging from labourers (employed on unskilled repetitive work) to 'sub-professionals' (mainly technicians and subordinate supervisors), managers and members of the professions. In the data for certain countries, farmers and rural workers are classified separately from industrial workers and persons engaged in other urban occupations. For one of the purposes of this study these categories were grouped into aggregates according to generally accepted criteria of low-level, medium-level and high-level occupations. Farmers, rural workers and unskilled labourers were classified in the low category, while clerical or sales and skilled manual workers were regarded as being in medium-level occupations. Occupations such as those requiring university or other tertiary education (e.g. 'sub-professionals', members of the professions, and persons occupying leading positions in public administration or private business) were arbitrarily classified at the high level.

Statistical Method

It is extremely difficult to make comparisons using elastic measures, as when one uses test data without knowing about the intricacies of tests and testing. To begin with, it must be realised that psychological tests have attributes that are variables in themselves. These attributes may confound the unwary reader. For example, a given test may have different reliabilities for different population groups of examinees. A test designed for high ability levels may not be very reliable for those at the low levels. Hence, direct comparisons of raw scores of different population groups on the same test often run into difficulties or give rise to unwarranted interpretations.

This pitfall is avoided by allowing for the elasticity of the measures after taking note of the spread, or variability, of the scores for each country. The achievement test data are broken down by occupational categories. We posit that $\bar{x}_i$ and $\bar{x}_j$ are the average achievement scores in the ith and the jth occupational categories, respectively, and σ_p is the standard deviation of the scores for the total population. Then we find the difference between the averages $\bar{x}_i$ and $\bar{x}_j$ and correct it for the spread of the population scores. We call this difference or distance (δ) in the following equation:

$$\delta_{ij} = (\bar{x}_i - \bar{x}_j)/\sigma_p, i \neq j.$$

The δs are expressed in standard deviation units, so that ability differences are indicated directly in those units. Thus, a δ of .5 means that the average scores of two groups being compared differ by one-half of the population standard deviation. If the tests are highly reliable and if the groups are very large, the δ need not be as large as that value to show a statistically significant difference: much smaller δs than .5 are shown by our calculations to be already statistically significant.[6]

For each country included in this study, we calculated the δs for four qualitative dimensions of thinking (cognitive) ability, namely (a) functional information, (b) comprehension, (c) application, and (d) higher mental processes. This was done first for the upper and lower levels of the occupational hierarchy, broadly defined, and then for the more specific occupational categories.

Observations by Countries

For a background, we summarise briefly here what has already been discovered with regard to the patterns of the δs from a few countries such as Australia, New Zealand and Sweden, which had been classified as advanced; we also compare those findings with those for Chile, a non-Asian country which had been classified as less developed.[7]

First, the δs between broad occupational categories, i.e. the high and the low major groups of parental occupations, are large. In Population II (fourteen-year-olds), they range from slightly less than one-half to slightly greater than one standard deviation. All these δs are at very high levels of statistical significance. The same observation holds true also for Population IV (pupils in their final year of pre-tertiary education), except that the δs in the latter are smaller.

Secondly, the δs tend to vary directly with the complexity of the ability tested. At the information and comprehension levels, they are already large; they tend to become larger towards the application level, sometimes up to the level of the higher mental processes. This tendency is markedly shown by Population II, between broad occupational categories; it becomes more marked between the extremes of the occupational hierarchy (e.g. between children of labourers and those of members of the professions) and much more so when a rural-urban difference is brought in (e.g. between children of farmers or rural workers and those of members of the professions). Again these observations appear to hold true for Population IV, except that the δs there are much smaller.

Thirdly, the δs decrease sharply from Population II to Population IV. Many of those in the latter are statistically trivial, indicating that the huge differences in test scores found in Population II are not found in Population IV. (This observation, however, tends to be true only for tests of low levels of ability; at the complex levels, e.g. application and the higher mental processes, some huge significant δs still remain.) Whether these decreases are due to special measures to level up the ability of children from the poor low occupational groups or simply to a brutal weeding out of those with low measured ability still needs to be ascertained.

Fourthly, all these observations apply not only to the countries classified as advanced but also to Chile, except that in Chile the patterns and tendencies of the δs are less pronounced.

India

As between the upper and lower levels of the occupational hierarchy in India,[8] the widest δ represented less than one-quarter of the population standard deviation.[9] Compared with the corresponding figures for the countries classified as advanced, these δs are quite narrow. Readers might thus be tempted to believe that in India the scholastic achievement of children is weakly associated with the occupation of parents. However, recalling the limitations of the data for India, we would rather defer strong interpretations until we see the patterns more clearly.

In respect of fourteen-year-olds (Population II) we see in Table 5.1 that for the broad categories (first line) the δs for information and comprehension levels are statistically significant although narrow. The trend is also rising up to the comprehension level, but there the rise stops, and the figures for the complex level of thinking faculty are not significant. The same pattern is also observable in the figures for children of unskilled workers by comparison with children of members of the professions, and the δ values derived from that comparison are larger. A greater magnification of the figures is shown by the line for children of large-scale farmers and fishery and forestry managers. Moreover, not only is the size of the δs greater but the gap is largest at a higher level for the farming group than for that of the unskilled workers. However, these observations rest on weak ground because, of the figures just mentioned, only those in the first two lines and columns are statistically significant. (The raw scores in India have such high variability that even if the differences are large, many δ figures are statistically insignificant.)

In respect of pupils in their last year of pre-tertiary education (Population IV, lines in italics), for unskilled workers we see significant gaps at the information and comprehension levels. The δs at the next two levels, however, are statistically trivial (even if signs are negative), which suggests that they are near zero. We can see also that the absolute values of the figures seem to decline in magnitude towards the more complex levels of ability.[10] The δs are much larger in the line for children of large-scale farmers than in the line for the children of unskilled workers. Some figures are statistically significant, and show that the children of the farmers did poorly in the test by scoring much lower than the children of unskilled workers. If these differences in scores indicate deprivation, then it would seem that children of farmers are more deprived than children of unskilled workers. Moreover, one must recognise that even for children of large-scale farmers, this observed gap is already considerable; and there is good reason to believe that children of small-scale farmers and of rural artisans are further down the scale.

A comparison can also be made among the changes in the δ values that occur between Population II (fourteen-year-olds) and Population IV (final year of pre-university education, which in India is supposed to be at the age of 16). From the figures in the table it seems that among children of unskilled workers the gaps tend to narrow as they move up into Population IV, except at the functional information level where the gap remains relatively wide. Among children of large-scale farmers, however, the gaps not only remain but also tend to widen, especially at the comprehension and application levels. There is, however, a tendency at the higher mental processes level for the observed gap to be dramatically reduced.[11]

Iran

In the analysis of the data from Iran we should at the outset be keenly aware that the test itself is a variable.

The δs between the upper and lower levels of the occupational hierarchy (Table 5.2) are of almost the same order of magnitude as those in India, and statistical significance was reached only at the application

Table 5.1: Achievement Disparities (δ) in India Between the Children of Parents in Different Occupations

Occupations of parents		Levels of mental ability tested			
		Functional information	Comprehension	Application	Higher mental processes
A. Broad categories (lower and upper levels of occupational hierarchy) — Pop. II		.183*	.237*	.121	.015
B. Specific occupations contrasted with the professions:					
Unskilled workers:	Pop. II	.398***	.440***	.280	.173
	Pop. IV	.408*	.211***	−.146	−.104
Large-scale farmers and fishery and forestry managers:	Pop. II	.380	.566	.967	.626
	Pop. IV	.393	.940*	.653**	−.063

*Significant at 1 per cent P (probability) level.
**Significant at 5 per cent P level.
***Significant at 10 per cent P level.

level of ability. What is important about this finding is that application is a complex form of mental ability, and that to be able to apply or use what they have learned already gives people a distinct advantage over others who cannot.

As we focus on the differences or gaps in specific occupational categories (e.g. between children of labourers and those of members of the professions), we find that the observed significant gap in the application level vanishes. However, a gap emerges at the functional information level among children of labourers and of semi-skilled and skilled workers, and at the comprehension level among children of carriage and cart-drivers, garbage men etc.[12] But among children of landholding farmers (i.e. owner-operators), no statistically significant δ was observed.

We would have expected that as we switched our analysis towards the specific occupational categories, the magnitudes of the gaps would become greater and the significant differences would tend to occur at more complex levels of ability, i.e. in Iran, to relate to the higher mental processes instead of to application. However, this was not so. Instead, significant δs occurred at the much lower levels: among

Table 5.2: Achievement Disparities (δ) in Iran Between the Children of Parents in Different Occupations

Occupations of parents		Levels of mental ability tested			
		Functional information	Comprehension	Application	Higher mental processes
A. Broad categories (lower and upper levels of occupational hierarchy) — Pop. II		.177	.121	.241**	.078
B. Specific occupations contrasted with the professions:					
Carriage and cart-drivers, garbage men etc.:	Pop. II	−.103	.500**	−.036	−.213
	Pop. IV	*−.105*	*−.011*	*.201*	*.401*
Labourers	Pop. II	.499**	.054	.162	.060
Semi-skilled and skilled workers	Pop. II	.315**	.115	.273	.030
Farmers (owner-operators)	Pop. II	.438	.017	.272	.146

**Significant at 5 per cent P level.

carriage and cart-drivers, garbage men etc., at comprehension level, and among labourers and semi-skilled and skilled workers at the functional information level. This seemingly inconsistent pattern seems likely to be one of the effects of the test as a variable itself. Owing to the high variability of the scores, a large n and a very wide δ are needed to reach statistically significant levels. Thus, what would have been a similar pattern to those of the other countries was observable only in the somewhat primitive forms of ability.

The traces of the pattern which were observed in other countries were also observable in Iran, although in the latter country statistical support is much weaker. Notice, for example, that the general tendency of the δs with regard to labourers seems to be towards smaller values, especially for the comprehension level, and the corresponding values in the third line of figures in the table are, in the strictly statistical sense, trivial: a gap that was found at the information level in Population II was virtually not observable in Population IV; this would mean that in Population IV there were no real gaps in the test responses between children of carriage and cart-drivers, garbage men etc. and those of members of the professions.

Thailand

Thailand seems to be an exceptional case. The very high variability of the scores makes it difficult to discern general patterns.[13]

Starting with the broad occupational categories,[14] we have difficulty in finding δs that are statistically significant. None the less, the figures from the information level to the higher mental processes level reveal a positive slope. If all these figures were statistically significant (at least at 5 per cent P level), then one could infer that the δs (representing real gaps) tend to widen towards the more complex levels of ability, a pattern that was observed in other countries. However, since these figures failed to reach statistically significant levels, this pattern may be regarded as only a faint trace of what may be real handicaps or gaps in Thailand.

Of the specific occupational categories, we use the category of craftsmen and skilled farmers,[15] and show that even at that level of the occupational hierarchy, some real gaps are likely to exist. The third line of figures in Table 5.3 seem to indicate that this observation is probably true at the functional information and comprehension levels. Among children of industrial workers this same observation seems to hold true at the very complex thinking level, i.e. higher mental processes (analysis, synthesis etc.). Whenever they tend to be significant the figures are much greater in the specific categories than in the broad ones, suggesting wider gaps in the former than in the latter.[16]

Table 5.3: Achievement Disparities (δ) in Thailand Between the Children of Parents in Different Occupations

Occupations of parents	Levels of mental ability tested			
	Functional information	Comprehension	Application	Higher mental processes
A. Broad categories (lower and upper levels of occupational hierarchy) — Pop. II	.109	.258	.249	.303***
B. Specific occupations contrasted with 'semi-professionals' and managerial personnel:				
Industrial workers: Pop. II	.610***	.052	−.563	.827**
Craftsmen and skilled farmers: Pop. II	.427**	.456**	.243	.190
Pop. IV	−.012	.162	.115	.025

**Significant at 5 per cent P level.
***Significant at 10 per cent P level.

With regard to Population IV, we have no line for industrial workers,[17] but we are able to show that between children of craftsmen and skilled farmers on the one hand and those of 'sub-professionals' and managers on the other, previous observable differences were reduced to the statistically trivial.

We do not know whether this shift from wide differences in Population II to near zero in Population IV is caused entirely by the test itself or by real differences which were virtually eliminated in the older samples. However, this observation should lead us to other plausible interpretations such as one that was made in the case of the developed countries.[18]

Common Features

After a country-by-country survey of achievement disparities, some common features can be identified.

The evidence shows that for the same age group (fourteen-year-olds), there are wide differences in achievement (test scores) between children of labourers (and related occupations) and the children of members of management and of the professions. More significantly, these differences have a qualitative dimension: they tend to become even more marked when the tests bear on complex thinking ability, with variations from one country to another as regards the particular level at which the difference is greatest (see Table 5.4).

Table 5.4: International Comparisons of Achievement Disparities (δ) in Populations II and IV Between the Children of Parents in Different Broad Occupational Categories

Level of mental ability	India		Iran		Thailand	
	Pop. II	Pop. IV	Pop. II	Pop. IV	Pop. II	Pop. IV
Functional information	.183*	.270*	.177	.158***	.109	−.465**
Comprehension	.237*	.086***	.121	.024	.258	.147
Application	.121	.002	.241**	.145***	.249	.384
Higher mental processes	.015	.032	.078	.116	.303***	.346

*Significant at 1 per cent P level.
**Significant at 5 per cent P level.
***Significant at 10 per cent P level.

The differences (δs) are even more marked when they are calculated with reference to smaller occupational categories falling within the major ones, e.g. between the children of particular categories of manual workers and those of members of the professions, or of management (Table 5.5). The differences are still greater when rural-urban contrasts are brought into the picture.

Table 5.5: International Comparisons of Achievement Disparities (δ) in Population II Between the Children of Parents in Different Specific Occupational Categories (Children of Various Categories of Manual Workers in Relation to Children of Members of the Professions or of Management)

Level of mental ability	India (unskilled workers)	Iran (labourers)	Thailand (skilled workers)
Functional information	.398***	.499***	.427**
Comprehension	.440***	.054	.456**
Application	.280	.162	.243
Higher mental processes	.173	.060	.190

**Significant at 5 per cent P level.
***Significant at 10 per cent P level.

In the final year of pre-university studies (Population IV), the differences (i.e. the δs) become smaller. But the qualitative differentiation seems to be persistent, for instance, with regard to functional information in India and higher mental processes in Iran. All these tendencies are observable not only between the children of labourers and those of professionals or managerial staff (Table 5.6) but also between the children of such staff and those of farmers and rural workers (see Table 5.7). These differences between specific occupational categories are generally reflected in differences between the broad occupational categories (Table 5.4), except in Thailand where the children of fathers in the 'low-level' occupations seem to do magnificently better than those in the top-level occupations at the functional information level. Why this is so is a puzzle which needs to be studied further.[19]

The fact that the δs are smaller in Population IV than in Population II can be attributed to the natural tendency for ability levels to become more uniform at the higher grades in the school system, with the degree of uniformity varying from one country to another. It was hinted earlier that this tendency could be due to the degree of selectivity of the school system or the efficiency of the schools in screening the less able pupils from the able. However, there could be several factors operating simultaneously on this result.

Table 5.6: International Comparisons of Achievement Disparities (δ) in Population IV Between the Children of Parents in Different Specific Occupational Categories (Children of Various Categories of Manual Workers in Relation to Children of Members of the Professions or of Management)

Level of mental ability	India (labourers)	Iran (semi-skilled workers)	Thailand (craftsmen and skilled farmers)
Functional information	.407*	.108	−.012
Comprehension	.211***	.090	.162
Application	−.146	.015	.115
Higher mental processes	−.104	.374**	.025

*Significant at 1 per cent P level.
**Significant at 5 per cent P level.
***Significant at 10 per cent P level.

Table 5.7: International Comparisons of Achievement Disparities (δ) in Population IV Between the Children of Parents in Different Specific Occupational Categories (Children of Farmers in Relation to Children of Members of the Professions or of Management)

Level of mental ability	India (large-scale farmers)	Iran (owner-operators)	Thailand
Functional information	.393	−.071	—
Comprehension	.940*	−.163	—
Application	.653**	.495	—
Higher mental processes	−.063	.204	—

*Significant at 1 per cent P level.
**Significant at 5 per cent P level.

One could imagine that from a given fixed point (e.g. 14-year-olds), countries have different downward gradients (or slopes) until the δs are virtually zero, and that countries would reach the 'zero gap' at different grade levels of schooling. It is also possible, though, that the slope is so small that the zero point is never reached within a reasonable period of schooling. This configuration is seen in δ_3 in Figure 5.1(a). This explanation assumes that the measurements were taken at two fixed points in time common to the countries under consideration, i.e. in the first instance at 14 years of age and in the next instance four years later; but that is not the case.

Figure 5.1: Hypothetical Explanations of Differences in the Achievement Disparities (β) in Populations II and IV

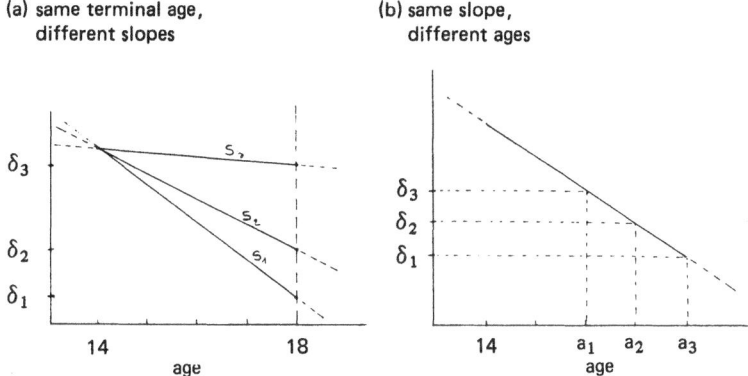

If the second measurement is taken at a fixed educational level, the ages vary.[20] The age distances between Populations II and IV in fact differ significantly among the countries included in this study: about three years in Thailand, almost five years in Iran, but only about two-and-a-half years in India. The age distances plus differences in selectivity could partly explain the reduction of the δs from Population II to Population IV. However, this hunch on selectivity has yet to be confirmed by statistical evidence; and it must not be forgotten that the test itself as a variable may have influenced the result as well.

Whatever the reasons, it is noteworthy that the gaps still exist in many of the countries in spite of selectivity. Selectivity merely hides the less able who, by implication, are usually the children of labourers and kindred workers. But why should such wide differences exist? Are not the ages or grade levels of these children the same?

We have studied the quantitative evidence which documents the wide qualitative differences in scholastic achievement among schoolchildren whose fathers have different occupations. This evidence was found in Australia, in New Zealand and in Sweden.[21] The same differences are also observable in Chile.[22] And in the Asian setting the same finding seems to hold true. In spite of the diversity in settings and conditions, the ubiquity of the disparities — like poverty — seems unassailable, even though the disparities vary in degree from one country to another.

To put it briefly, test performances reveal that, on the average, children of labourers and kindred workers are apt to have a 'less developed' thinking faculty than children of members of the professions and of management. This contrast becomes even sharper when a rural-urban distinction is made. At the lowest level of the ability scale, i.e. functional information, large differences already exist; and these differences increase towards the more complex levels of ability, i.e. in comprehension, application and higher mental processes.

For many readers, this finding will probably confirm general impressions. Children of labourers and the poor in general do not have access to as much schooling as the children of the rich: hence the difference in the development of their thinking ability. But these findings hold in spite of the same age or same grade level.

The observations based on fourteen-year-old schoolchildren appear to hold true also among young people in the final year of pre-university studies, which in many countries means pupils with more than twelve years of schooling. Even though in the older samples the gaps tend to be reduced somewhat, they are still wide and noticeable, especially in the less developed countries. This tendency could be merely an effect of selectivity and other factors which, by attrition, cause the less able to drop out of school. Thus, what might be called a narrowing of the gap may well not be a real gain caused by positive measures.

There were specific variations of the general finding from country to country and from one level of economic development to another. There were also observations which do not fit neatly into the general picture. But none of these variations and discrepancies impair the general finding that even with the same age or grade level, there are wide disparities in thinking ability between children of labourers and rural workers and those of members of the professions and of management. This finding goes to show that even if students have the same school certificates or the same length of schooling, they have no semblance of equality in thinking ability, nor in other substantive terms, on the average. If this proposition is indeed true it casts serious doubt on the orthodox policy of merely equalising the length of schooling as a means of redistributing education, much less as a means of redistributing future income.

Notes

1. The data utilised in this chapter were made available by the International Association for the Evaluation of Educational Achievement (IEA) through its repository in Stockholm. No responsibility for the analysis or interpretations presented here is to be attributed to the IEA, the original collectors of the data or the IEA repository. A serious consideration of the results reported in this chapter requires a reasonable degree of acquaintance with the methods used by the IEA to conduct the international evaluation exercise. We therefore suggest that interested readers should consult Gilbert F. Peaker, *An Empirical Study of Education in Twenty-One Countries: A Technical Report* (Stockholm, Almquist and Wiksell International, 1975).

2. In combination with traits in the affective domain (attitudes, values etc.) see David R. Krathwohl et al., *Taxonomy of Educational Objectives. Handbook II: Affective Domain* (New York, David McKay, 1964).

3. A few of the recent theoretical developments in this area are: Hartog's 'capability variables', Lydall's 'I and D factors', Tinbergen's thoughts on leadership and independence, Welch's 'allocative ability' and Schultz's 'ability to deal with disequilibria'. Obviously, these human qualities transcend general mental ability and such summary measures as IQ scores. See the following specific references: Joop Hartog, 'Ability and Age-Income Profiles', *The Review of Income and Wealth*, Series 22, No. 1 (March 1976), pp. 61-74; Harold Lydall, 'Theories of the Distribution of Earnings' in A.B. Atkinson (ed.), *The Personal Distribution of Incomes* (London, George Allen and Unwin, 1976), pp. 15-46; Jan Tinbergen, 'Personal Characteristics and Income' in Atkinson, *Distribution of Incomes*; Finis Welch, 'Education in Production', *The Journal of Political Economy*, Vol. 78 (January-February 1970), pp. 35-59; T.W. Schultz, 'The Value of Ability to Deal with Disequilibria', *The Journal of Economic Literature*, Vol. XIII, No. 3 (September 1975), pp. 827-46.

4. Namely, functional information, comprehension, application and higher mental processes (such as analysis and synthesis). See Benjamin S. Bloom (ed.), *Taxonomy of Educational Objectives. Handbook I: Cognitive Domain* (New York, Longmans, Green and Co., 1956).

5. Peaker, *An Empirical Study*.

6. δ is amenable to testing for statistical significance by merely replacing the standard deviation by the standard error of the difference with Ho: $u_i - u_j = o$. A similar result would be obtained by F-tests in analysis of variance. The use of δ avoids reporting on raw score averages which might engender invidious comparisons among countries.

7. See M.D. Leonor Jr, *Patterns of Inequality in Education in Asia*, Part I, World Employment Programme research working paper (restricted) (Geneva, ILO), pp. 48-59.

8. The lower level of the occupational hierarchy comprises unskilled workers, farm labourers and semi-skilled workers. The upper level consists of 'sub-professionals' (e.g. primary school teachers), managerial executives and professional people (e.g. principals of colleges, engineers, architects, jurists).

9. In Australia, New Zealand and Sweden, the δs ranged from a little over 0.5 to over 1 standard deviation unit.

10. This decline is partly due to the nature of the test. At those levels the test items are probably becoming so much more difficult that ability differences between groups of schoolchildren are difficult to detect.

11. See note 10.

12. This is the lowest occupational category in Iran.

13. The occupational classification of the data on Thailand is not readily comparable with others.

14. The low group is composed of day labourers, service personnel (e.g. domestic servants, hotel workers and industrial workers); the top group consists of 'semi-professionals' and managerial personnel and members of the professions, defined as 'any career that requires at least four years of training at the university level', e.g. judges, doctors of medicine, engineers. See *IEA Six-Subject Data Bank Manual*, File M2002, p. 241.

15. From the intermediate group.

16. This feature could be due entirely to aggregation: when the figures are disaggregated the differences appear more sharply. Moreover, we are trying to uncover a rural dimension by the addition of 'skilled farmers'; this may lead to a wider gap. But at this point, we must underline the fact that we have no information on which of the two (i.e. children of craftsmen or of skilled farmers) have the higher scores on the average.

17. Due to the small n we did not analyse this survey.

18. An apparent levelling up of abilities is perhaps due not to remedial measures but to selectivity, which simply gets rid of the less able.

19. It is suspected that this could be due to the interplay of several factors, namely (a) imprecise classification of the occupation; (b) sampling, i.e. many children of top professional people may be in exclusive schools not included in the sample; (c) natural tendency of the children of top professional people towards 'non-science' careers, while career opportunities in science are more attractive to children of the 'labouring' class; and (d) the test as a variable itself.

20. We must be aware that these measurements are cross-sectional, i.e. at the same time but in different population groups, as a means to infer a longitudinal development.

21. Leonor, *Patterns of Inequality*.

22. Note, however, that these findings apply only to pupils who have remained in school. If the abilities of school drop-outs were accounted for, which the data do not permit, the observed differences could be much greater.

6 DETERMINANTS OF EDUCATIONAL ACHIEVEMENT IN THE PHILIPPINES

Previous studies have shown that differences in scholastic achievement among schoolchildren are due to differences in background factors between students, schools, countries and, as we have shown, between categories of countries at different stages of economic development. At this point, it is perhaps sufficient to show within-country disparities as a first step toward a logical explanation of such differences.

In this chapter the notion of results is used to compare educational parity or disparity between units. Of course results have many forms, ranging from sophisticated psychometric measures to such crude (but none the less readily available) information as proportions of age groups completing a level of schooling or achieving a skill such as literacy. For the same unit of analysis (population group), parity or disparity is evaluated on the basis of differences in measures of access, level of schooling completed, and specific abilities acquired. Our analysis refers to groups or aggregates. This is because while it is extremely difficult to achieve parity of results for all individuals, it should be less so for groups.

One primary point here concerns access. It is often argued that access to schools is merely a matter of availability of seats in those schools. This view implies that simply by increasing the number of those seats the problem of access is solved. This, of course, is far from the truth. Attendance requires a financial capacity of households to send their children there instead of letting them drop out soon for economic reasons. But even if financial circumstances change dramatically the problem of access is very far from solved, especially at higher levels of schooling. Access defined in terms of admission and successful completion of schooling is contingent not only on financial capacity but also on ability, particularly scholastic ability, and other factors. Ability is not developed instantly, it is painstakingly acquired through the years.

Conditions of deprivation caused by severely low household income for prolonged periods, especially during the pupils' early years, are bound to leave their scars on scholastic achievement. Thus, in a keenly competitive activity such as schooling, pupils from deprived backgrounds tend to be almost always the losers. These notions are explored

80 *Educational Achievement in the Philippines*

empirically with data from the Philippines.

This chapter begins by looking at the broad contours of educational achievement, particularly in school attendance, including the sex and regional disparities. It then focuses on the results of the National College Entrance Examination (NCEE), comparing them with the test results at the primary school level (Project SOUTELE).[1] Finally, admission to the University of the Philippines, a highly subsidised state educational institution, is considered. The main thrust of the analysis is: what determines scholastic achievement as a basis for access? What is abundantly clear in these cases is that household income appears as a prominent determinant of scholastic achievement and a requirement for admission and for streaming towards high-income occupations.

Broad Contours of Educational Achievement

The Philippines is probably a special case among the countries of the region. The literacy rate is high, female attendance at school is high, and the country also ranks high in terms of post-high-school attendance per unit of population.[2]

Literacy

Sex difference in literacy[3] for the entire country is so very small that one can safely say that females have almost achieved parity with males. This gap is even narrower in urban than in rural areas. As between rural and urban areas the difference in literacy rates is wider, i.e. about 15 percentage points; it is somewhat wider among females (15.66) than among males (14.65).

Table 6.1: Literacy Rate (Six Years and Older), Philippines, 1970

	(Per cent)			*Male-female difference*
	All	Male	Female	
All	76.39	76.90	75.90	*1.00*
Urban	86.60	86.95	86.29	*0.66*
Rural	71.47	72.30	70.63	*1.67*
Urban-rural difference	*15.13*	*14.65*	*15.66*	

Source: Calculated from Philippines *Census of Population and Housing*, 1970.

Attendance Rates

On the whole, however, attendance rates are slightly better for males than for females, particularly in the urban areas; in rural areas the attendance rate of females seems better than that of the males. The figures also show (Table 6.2) that differences in attendance rates between the sexes within regions are much less than the differences between regions within the same sex. These figures can be expressed more sharply by using the notion of gaps[4] and by bringing into the picture a distinction between Manila, where the way of life is modern, and the provinces.[5]

Table 6.2: Regional and Sex Differences in School Attendance Rates (Six Years and Older), Philippines, 1970*

	All	Urban	Rural	Urban-rural difference	*Gaps*
Philippines	28.07	32.45	25.96	6.50	*25.04*
Male	28.32	33.62	25.89	7.73	*29.86*
Female	27.81	31.38	26.03	5.35	*20.55*
Male-female difference	0.51	2.24	0.14		
Gaps	*1.83*	*7.14*	*0.54*		

*School attendance rates are indicated by the percentage of the population attending school.
Source: Calculated from census.

Table 6.3: Regional and Sex Gaps in School Attendance Rates (Six Years and Older), Philippines, 1970

	Philippines	Manila	Provinces	Regional Difference	*Gaps*
All	28.07	34.98	27.79	7.19	*25.87*
Male	28.32	36.60	28.01	8.59	*30.67*
Female	27.81	33.50	27.58	5.92	*21.46*
Male-female difference	0.51	3.10	0.43		
Gaps	*1.83*	*9.25*	*1.56*		

Source: Calculated from census.

The general impression from both Tables 6.2 and 6.3 is that regional gaps are much wider than the gaps referring to sex differences in attendance rates. In particular, regional gaps are wider among males than among females. Within the same region, e.g. in the provinces and in

82 *Educational Achievement in the Philippines*

rural areas, sex parity in attendance rates seems almost achieved. This is, however, far from being the case in Manila and other urban areas, where males had much better attendance rates than the females.

Scholastic Achievement in Terms of Measured Results

Attendance rates are a measure, however crudely, of access to schools. But access is only a preliminary step.[6] More important is what has been learned, the outcomes of schooling. These are myriad, and tracking down all of them is extremely difficult. Fortunately, however, some indirect evidence of these outcomes is sometimes available.

At a low level of scholastic achievement,[7] i.e. passing a national test for admission to further education after high school — the National College Entrance Examination (NCEE) — we find no evidence that there is a sex-related difference in test performance. Table 6.4 suggests that if such a difference exists at all, we would have to look for it elsewhere, possibly at the high levels of scholastic ability.[8]

Table 6.4: Percentage Distribution of Male and Female Examinees Passing the National College Entrance Examination, by Region, 1973

Regions	Male	Female
Manila and suburbs	21.62	21.43
Ilocos — Mountain Province	5.74	6.22
Cagayan Valley	3.56	3.42
Central Luzon	15.56	14.46
Southern Luzon and islands	13.41	13.85
Bicol	5.16	4.94
West Visayas	9.57	10.17
Central Visayas	6.65	6.61
East Visayas	3.49	3.70
North Mindanao	5.78	5.87
South Mindanao	9.05	8.90

$\chi^2 = 0.2034$. Not significant.
Source: NCEE.

Regional Differences (or Disparities) in Scholastic Achievement

We now show that there are regional disparities in scholastic achievement as indicated by the NCEE results in 1973. At the apex of this ability are students who came from Manila and suburbs. Their ability level is significantly higher than that of high school leavers from the provinces.

Table 6.5: Mean Scores of General Scholastic Aptitude*

	Mean	Coefficient of variation
Philippines	480.77	13.04
Manila	512.64	14.34
Provinces	473.34	12.76
Difference	*39.30***	

*The score is an average of scores of subtests in symbolic verbal relations, abstract reasoning, English, mathematics and science. The first two are tests of mental ability, while the last three are subject proficiency tests. The standard scores have a mean of 500 and a standard deviation of 100.
**Significance greater than 1 per cent P (probability) level.
Source: NCEE.

The high scholastic achievement of students from Manila is accompanied by a somewhat greater variability, which suggests that the spread of such ability is wider there than in the provinces.

A region-by-region comparison of achievement levels reveals tremendous differences. However, Ilocos, the Mountain Provinces and Bicol have similar mean scores of general scholastic aptitude; likewise Central Luzon, West Visayas and Southern Mindanao are on the same level of scholastic achievement. For these last three regions and East Visayas, the mean scores of general scholastic aptitude are so low that they can be regarded as scholastically deprived areas. It is probably no mere coincidence that they are also currently trouble spots in the Philippines: that situation is probably a consequence of scholastic and other forms of relative deprivation.

The high scores of high school leavers from Manila and suburbs are reflected in high scores in the subtests of the National College Entrance Examination. The better scores were not only in the mental ability tests (e.g. symbolic verbal relations and abstract reasoning) but also — and much higher — in subject proficiency tests in English, mathematics and science. This high performance seems to be accompanied by a certain degree of variability which is a little higher in the subject proficiency tests than in the mental ability tests. The same pattern of variability, although at a somewhat lower level, also appears among the scores of pupils from the provinces.

These findings on the level of test performance appear consistent with the contrasts between countries classified as advanced and less developed respectively in the IEA studies.

If we accept the proposition that Manila and suburbs generally have better schools (e.g. better qualified teachers, better facilities and

Table 6.6: Regional Differences in Mean Scores for General Scholastic Aptitude

Regions	Means	(1)	(2)	(3)	(4)	(5)	(6)	(7)	(8)	(9)	(10)
(1) Manila and suburbs	512.62										
(2) Ilocos – Mountain Province	480.54	32.10									
(3) Cagayan and Batanes	465.93	46.71	14.61								
(4) Central Luzon	470.30	42.34	10.24	– 4.37							
(5) Southern Luzon and islands	478.46	34.18	2.08	–12.53	– 8.16						
(6) Bicol	480.70	31.94	– 0.16*	–14.77	–10.40	– 2.24					
(7) West Visayas	470.76	41.88	9.78	– 4.83	– 0.46*	7.70	9.94				
(8) Central Visayas	488.94	23.70	– 8.40	–23.01	–18.64	–10.48	– 8.24	–18.18			
(9) East Visayas	460.55	52.09	19.19	5.38	9.75	17.91	20.15	10.21	28.39		
(10) North Mindanao	463.21	49.43	17.33	2.72	7.09	15.25	17.49	7.55	25.73	– 2.66	
(11) South Mindanao	471.05	41.59	9.49	– 5.12	0.75*	7.41	9.65	– 0.29*	17.89	–10.50	– 7.84

*Non-significant difference. All other differences between mean scores are significant beyond the 1 per cent probability level.
Source: Calculations from data supplied by the NCEE.

learning conditions), richer non-school learning opportunities and better home conditions than the provinces, it is likely that these differences have systematic effects on the disparities and variabilities of scholastic achievement.[9] This observation strongly suggests that schooling (as well as other educational factors) differentiates people, and that the better the schooling is the greater the differentiation. Also, the chances are that the more uneven the distribution of the schooling, the more uneven will the differentiation be, especially when the better pupils tend to receive more of the educational resources.[10]

Table 6.7: Regional Differences in Levels and Variability of NCEE Subscores, 1973

Area	Means				
	SVR	AR	English	Mathematics	Science
Philippines	485.01	567.00	455.69	462.95	434.43
Manila	512.79	591.94	491.61	500.01	468.87
Provinces	478.54	562.15	447.32	454.31	426.39
Difference	*34.25**	*29.79**	*44.29**	*45.70**	*42.48**
Difference (%)	*7.16*	*5.30*	*9.90*	*10.06*	*9.96*
	Coefficients and variations				
	SVR	AR	English	Mathematics	Science
Philippines	15.44	11.78	18.84	18.52	18.15
Manila	16.00	11.22	20.59	19.02	19.27
Provinces	15.30	11.90	19.23	17.37	17.88
Difference	*0.70*	*−0.68*	*1.36*	*1.65*	*1.39*
Difference (%)	*4.58*	*−5.71*	*7.07*	*9.50*	*7.77*

*Significance beyond 1 per cent P level.
Key: SVR = symbolic verbal relations.
     AR = abstract reasoning.
Source: NCEE.

Further Results of the National College Entrance Examination (NCEE)

We can explore and expand this analysis of the NCEE by analysing the factors which influence its score of general scholastic aptitude.[11] We can take the regional mean and the regional variance of the NCEE and regress them on regional data on adult literacy and on the mean and variance of household incomes in logarithms.

Adult literacy was measured as the proportion of the population 25 years old or older (in 1970) who had completed at least secondary school. It was hypothesised that the presence of highly literate adults confers neighbourhood effects (externalities) on community life (largely outside schools) which enrich learning opportunities and improve the scholastic achievement of pupils.

Income level was indicated by monthly income (in pesos) of the household from which the pupil came. Given the number of pupils from each income class, the mean household income (in logarithms) was estimated for each province. From the same grouped data, the *variance* was likewise calculated. The income level reflects to some degree the available resources in the pupil's home; to a certain extent it is also a more general indicator about the home.

The *variance of household incomes* in logarithms measures the concentration of income. In this case (and at the province level), we are examining the effects of the distribution of income (among households included in the study) on scholastic achievement.

The model we used for the analysis is as follows:

$$Y_0 = f(X_1, X_2, X_3; D); \quad (1)$$
$$\text{and} \quad Y_1 = f(X_1, X_2, X_3; D); \quad (2)$$

The level of scholastic achievement (Y_0) associated with the province is influenced by the educational level (X_1) of its adult population, by their level of incomes (X_2), by the concentration (X_3), or distribution, of those incomes among households of pupils and by unmeasured variables which tend to be peculiar to regions (D). In equation (2), the variability (Y_1) of scholastic achievement is merely substituted for Y_0 to test the hypothesis that the same variables ($X_1, \ldots, X_2, D$) also affect 'the spread' or distribution of that scholastic achievement.

Findings

In well-specified regression equations, the standardised coefficients normally indicate the effect of the independent variables on the dependent variable. In strictly mathematical terms, each of the coefficients is an estimate of the effect of a variable on the dependent variable when the other variables in the equation are held constant. However, the precision of such estimates is contingent on a number of factors. One of them is that the independent variables are truly independent, e.g., that their intercorrelations are statistically zero. Otherwise, the coefficients as estimates will be untrustworthy and misleading.

The independent variables we have used are, to some degree, inevitably intercorrelated. For instance, communities (or provinces) which have a high density of literate persons tend to be also those with high levels of income, although we are not sure of the effect of this on the level of the income inequality. Having this forewarning, we designed regression statements that would allow us to interpret the effects of the variables in a hierarchical way, i.e. the contribution of an 'independent' variable (to the variance explained) net of those already in the equation. So, here we relied not only on the estimates of the standardised regression coefficients but also on the change in the R^2 contributed by a variable in a predetermined sequence.

Our estimates (Table 6.8) show that the income level of parents has a significant effect on the test performance of their children, and that the variance of this income level seems to be of little significance. Adult literacy (of the province as a unit of analysis) appears also to be of minor importance. However, D_1 as the dummy variable for Luzon (as a region) exhibited a large regression coefficient at a high level of significance. These observations from the coefficients are confirmed by the relative sizes of the change in R^2. Interpreted in another way, the income level of parents contributed about 47.5 per cent and D_1 about 30 per cent to the total variance explained ($R^2 = .40$). This suggests that having high-income parents and studying in Luzon are important to achieving high test performance.

The available data do not permit us to show why these observations are the way they are. But common-sense impressions do tell us that high-income households tend to have most of the things that are often wanting in low-income homes (e.g. better food and nutrition, more books and other reading materials, longer study time) and that are in sum generally conducive to learning. Furthermore, there is nothing sacred about the dummy variable for Luzon. It seems to indicate that Luzon as a geographical area is different from the Visayas and Mindanao and that the situation in the former promotes high test performance. Our suspicion is that the educational infrastructure in Luzon is much better, generally speaking, than those of the other regional divisions of the country. This is likely true, too, in terms of the general level of socio-economic development, even if there could be pockets of exceptions.

In the second equation, i.e. with Y_1 (or the standard deviation of general scholastic aptitude) as the dependent variable, it was found that only the adult literacy level of the province was statistically significant; the rest of the independent variables were nearly trivial.[12] (See

Table 6.8: Effects of Some Factors on Test Performance in the NCEE, 1973

	$\hat{\beta}$	Change in R^2	Relative contribution (per cent)
Ave. of ln household income	.31**	.19	47.5
Adult literacy	.13	.04	10.0
Variance of ln income	.12	.03	7.5
D_1 (Luzon)	.47*	.12	30.0
D_2 (Visayas)[a]	.18	.02	5.0
Total		.40	100.0
Adj. R^2 = .35	F = 8.13		df = 5/60

*Significant at 1 per cent P level.
**Significant at 5 per cent P level.
[a]D_3 (Mindanao) is the excluded category.

Table 6.9: Effects of Some Variables on the Variability of Test Performance in the NCEE, 1973

	$\hat{\beta}$	Change in R^2	Relative contribution (per cent)
Adult literacy	.47*	.13	75.58
Average of ln household income	−.19	.02	11.63
Variance of ln household income	.03	.001	0.58
D_3 (Mindanao)	.16	.02	11.63
D_2 (Visayas)[a]	.03	.001	0.58
Total		.172	100.00
Adj. R^2 = .10	F = 2.42		df = 5/60

*Significant at 1 per cent P level.
[a]D_1 (Luzon) is the excluded category.

Table 6.9.) The small total R^2 seems to reveal that there are variables other than those in the equation which could explain more significantly the variations or the spread of the test scores, at the province level of analysis.

We investigated this hypothesis in the following analysis (Table 6.10), and found that in the somewhat better developed regions, e.g. Luzon, incomes depended more and more on the educational levels of the heads or parents of the pupils' households.[13] Hence, once either of the two, i.e. income or adult literacy, is entered into the equation, the other becomes insignificant. Curiously, however, the X_3 (variance of ln income) assumes a negative coefficient (at low statistical levels); this suggests that high variability of household incomes tends to be associated with a low average scholastic achievement level of pupils.

In Mindanao (where household incomes seem to be not too heavily dependent on schooling), X_1 (adult literacy) has a virtually insignificant effect on Y_0 (general scholastic aptitude) but the level of income of the household seems to compensate for this. In fact, the influence of the latter appears to be quite substantial. What this finding seems to suggest is that in the developed regions the educational level of the population tends to exert a powerful influence on the scholastic achievement of pupils, and that in the less developed regions the income level of the household becomes a more important determinant of that achievement.

Table 6.10: Effect of Adult Literacy and Household Income Level on Scholastic Achievement of Students, NCEE 1973, Luzon and Mindanao

	Luzon[a]	Mindanao
X_1 (Adult literacy)	0.43**	−0.04
X_2 (ln income)	−	0.84**
X_3 (Variance ln income)	−	−0.07
Adj R^2	0.16	0.52
F	6.30	7.08
df	1/27	3/14

**Significant at 5 per cent P level.
[a]Luzon less its southern islands.

We have thus shown that household income has a large effect on general scholastic aptitude. Likewise, residing or studying in Luzon or in the economically developed provinces has a similar or even larger effect on that aptitude.

However, while these factors influenced the general level of scholastic aptitude, they did not seem to affect the pattern or the spread of that aptitude. Instead, adult literacy as previously defined had the largest and most significant effect on that spread, suggesting that adult literacy as a community factor contributed much to the differentiation of scholastic ability.

Evidence from Project SOUTELE

SOUTELE is an acronym for survey of outcomes of elementary education. Project SOUTELE is a national survey of learning outcomes conducted in 1975 by the Department (now Ministry) of Education and Culture. It produced a series of studies which provide insights into the problem of access and into the mechanisms which reproduce the disparities that emerge in the NCEE and other examinations preparatory to further schooling. Under the project a non-verbal mental ability test and a battery of achievement tests were developed and administered to a national sample of about 28,000 pupils in Grades V and VI, to assess what had been learnt by the pupils in the various subjects taught in Philippine elementary schools.[14] The results of this survey were published in 1976 by the Ministry through its Educational Development Projects Implementing Task Force (EDPITAF).[15]

The object of the analysis here is to show in more detail than in the previous chapters the strong association between socio-economic background and educational achievement, particularly during the last two years of the pupil's elementary or basic schooling in the Philippines. The analysis starts with a brief description of test performance, followed by an analysis of this result to show its dynamic aspect, i.e. the rate of progress, leading us to the factors which can influence achievement. Then a supposed causal chain of these factors is described in turn.

The results were reported by type of schools; accordingly, our analysis follows this typology, which is based on school location and source of funding. The types are: (a) 'barrio' schools, (b) central schools and (c) private schools. The barrio schools are schools in the villages (barrios) which are in unmistakably rural areas. Several barrios together constitute a *municipio*, whose market or political centre is the *poblacion* where the central and private schools are located. Both barrio and central schools are supported by state funds. A private school, like a central school, is also located in a *poblacion*, but it is funded by private money, e.g. by tuition and other fees that parents pay to the school directly. Test performance results in Table 6.11 show clearly that in grade VI private schools on average out-perform central schools which in turn do better than barrio schools. In grade V the private schools' lead is lost although barrio schools still follow the others.[16]

Achievement in One School Year: the Rate of Progress

Reports issued under the SOUTELE project have shown that sixth-graders score consistently higher than fifth-graders in the scholastic achievement tests. It is noted in the reports that the differences are small even if they are statistically significant, and it is stated that this significance may be mainly due to a large sample size. In our view, however, this result is probably due to other factors. In fact, under the

SOUTELE project an attempt was made to investigate several other hypotheses concerning the small increment in overall scores in one school year, suggesting the possibilities of enlarging that increment by several if-statements. However, our interest in this study does not lie in why the increment referred to above is large or small on the whole. We prefer to investigate such questions as why does pupil performance on the tests differ among, for instance, the types of schools? Why is the hierarchy of scores consistent among Grade VI pupils and not among Grade Vs? And why are the supposed above-mentioned advantages of private schools over central schools not shown by the latter over barrio schools especially when the increments are measured in rates of percentage change?

Table 6.11: Achievement Test Performance of Grade V and VI Pupils by Type of Schools

Subjects	Barrio schools	Central schools	Private schools
Grade VI			
Reading	13.70	16.70	21.62
Science	21.23	24.87	22.42
Mathematics	13.27	14.50	17.03
Social Studies	13.13	14.91	16.96
Language	24.77	28.29	35.43
Pagbasa	20.46	23.40	27.18
Wika	28.35	31.45	35.35
Work Education	11.12	12.22	14.02
Home Economics	13.20	15.31	16.17
Grade V			
Reading	11.60	15.90	15.12
Science	18.73	23.57	29.72
Mathematics	11.57	12.70	11.03
Social Studies	10.53	13.21	10.46
Language	23.67	28.49	30.63
Pagbasa	17.46	22.60	19.78
Wika	25.95	30.55	29.95
Work Education	8.52	11.32	10.12
Home Economics	9.20	13.21	10.47

Source: SOUTELE, Vol. 1 (Technical Report), Table 66, pp. 300-1, and Vol. 2, Table 3.4.

The mean percentage score differences between the fifth and sixth grades are larger for barrio schools than for central schools, although those for private schools are much larger. By transforming these figures into percentage changes, the unevenness of the score increments among types of schools is highlighted (Table 6.12). Notice, for example, that the 'incremental change'[17] in the test performance of pupils in village schools is higher than that of those in central schools — all of which are public or government-supported schools. This finding seems contrary to general expectations, i.e. that the rates of change ought to be faster in central schools than in barrio schools, as they are in private schools; or, simply but less precisely, that a high score in Grade V would be associated with a high score increment in Grade VI.[18]

Table 6.12: Rates of Change* in Test Performance After One School Year Between Grade V and Grade VI

Subject	Barrio	Central	Private
Reading	18.10	5.03	42.99
Language	4.45	− 0.70	15.67
Pagbasa	17.18	3.54	37.41
Wika	9.25	2.95	18.03
Science	13.35	5.52	32.56
Mathematics	14.69	14.17	54.40
Social Studies	24.69	12.87	62.14
Work Education	30.52	7.95	38.54
Home Economics	43.48	15.90	54.44

*Given by the formula $((S_6 - S_5)/S_5)\,100$ where S_5 = score in Grade V; S_6 = score in Grade VI.
Source: Calculated from SOUTELE, Vol. 1, Table 3.4, and Vol. 2, Table 66.

Correlates

As a step towards explaining the systematic variation of test performance, e.g. the rank order and differences of average scores between types of schools, we describe below certain variables which are associated with educational achievement.

Community Background. This follows strictly the location of schools. The rural-urban typology of schools represents a set of factors which interact with school factors. The chances are — and this is a conjecture — that each set may have a significant association with test performance, plus the mutually reinforcing effects of both. In the negative sense, for example, deprived learning conditions in villages matched by deprived situations in barrio schools (due, for example, to less qualified teachers, bad library facilities, poor supervision) can — as generally believed — have deleterious effects on pupils.

Parental Background. This is almost the same as home background. We

Educational Achievement in the Philippines

split this variable into two elements, namely *income level* and *schooling* of parents, and show that they have a high degree of association with test performance.

Income Level. From the tabulated data published under the SOUTELE project, we calculated the average incomes of parents of pupils going to the different types of elementary schools. At the lowest end of the income scale (394 pesos) are parents who send their children to barrio schools, followed by the parents of children in the central schools (555 pesos) with, at the apex, the parents who patronise the private schools (705 pesos). The same hierarchy is also observed in the averages of test scores in Grade VI in all subjects except science.[19] This is true even in 'practical' subjects such as work education for boys and home economics for girls.

Schooling. Reports issued under the SOUTELE project indicate the distribution of parents by schooling. The figures show (Table 6.13) that the amount of schooling received by parents is lowest among those who send their children to barrio schools. Next are the parents of children in central schools and then those of children in the private schools. The rank order of magnitudes applies not only to parents of children in Grade V but also to those of children in Grade VI.

Table 6.13: Schooling of Parents (ratios of weighted sums*)

	Barrio schools	Central schools	Private schools
Grade V	*1.00*	*1.47*	*1.94*
Father	1.00	1.50	1.90
Mother	1.00	1.43	1.99
Grade VI	*1.00*	*1.33*	*1.94*
Father	1.00	1.33	1.91
Mother	1.00	1.33	1.98

*The weights are as follows: no schooling = 0; did not finish elementary course = 3; finished elementary course = 6; did not finish high school = 8; finished high school = 10; attended some years in college = 12; finished college = 14; master's or professional degree = 16; doctorate, including doctor of medicine = 18.

Mass Media Exposure. Under Project SOUTELE pupils were asked how often they engaged in certain activities, and the frequencies of response to this subjective question were reported. We summarised these data in Table 6.14, and show that observable differences in exposure to mass media exist among pupils who studied in different types of schools. We note that pupils in the barrio schools tended to have the least exposure. The differences between the figures for these schools and those of the central schools seem small, but they are generally large between the central schools and the private schools, and are much larger between the barrio schools and the latter.[20]

Table 6.14: Frequency of Exposure to Mass Media*

Grade and medium	Barrio schools	Central schools	Private schools
Grade V			
Radio	154.6	156.1	141.0
Television	86.5	116.4	166.9
Cinema	93.3	116.6	136.8
Daily newspapers	110.3	136.7	138.6
Weekly magazines	119.2	142.7	146.0
Comic books or magazines	158.5	188.2	216.2
Children's books	160.1	193.7	199.8
Grade VI			
Radio	153.7	157.5	157.3
Television	96.8	116.8	205.0
Cinema	97.6	114.9	144.6
Daily newspapers	120.6	137.9	171.2
Weekly magazines	125.7	145.3	164.4
Comic books or magazines	166.8	197.9	229.6
Children's books	159.2	180.6	204.2

*Weighted sums. The weights are: never = 0; sometimes = 1; often = 3; very often =5.
Source: Calculated from SOUTELE, Vol. 1, Tables 59-C and 59-D, pp. 220-1.

Mental Ability. For assessing the general mental development of children in the elementary schools, without too much bias towards subject matter and language, Project SOUTELE constructed a non-verbal mental ability test. The test was designed to cover the following processes: association, analogy, classification, visual acuity, spatial relationships and abstract reasoning. The estimated reliability of the entire test is 0.90, a fairly high coefficient for a group test.

The results of this test show even more striking differences among pupils studying in the different types of schools reported under the SOUTELE project. Table 6.15 indicates 'that among the three institution types, the private schools got the highest mean; the barrio schools, the lowest mean'.[21] Analysis of the differences in mean scores revealed that the differences are at high levels of statistical significance.

Table 6.15: Mental Ability Test Data of Grade VI Pupils in Three Types of Elementary Schools (based on a 10% sample)

	Barrio schools	Central schools	Private schools
Mean	48.85	52.62	61.54
Std. deviation	12.79	14.49	13.00
N	977	871	431

Significance of the difference	Difference	SE diff	t	Significance
Central-barrio	3.77	.64	5.9	.01
Private-central	8.92	.80	11.15	.01
Private-barrio	12.69	.75	16.92	.01

Source: SOUTELE, Vol. 1, Tables 68 and 69, p. 305.

This recital of the correlates develops an impression that the children in barrio schools seem to differ from the children in the other schools on almost all counts. They are supposed to have completed the same grade level and yet one feels that they are widely different even in skills that are supposed to have been developed by the schools.

A Causal Paradigm

It can be supposed that all the correlates are associated with each other in such a way that the reciprocal influences would be hopelessly difficult to disentangle. However, we can utilise the principle of weak ordering of these variables in order to construct a tentative, hypothetical causal chain among them.

Weak ordering assumes that some variable may affect another but not the other way round.[22] Among correlates, this ordering is established by time precedence, i.e. the supposed cause must precede the supposed effect; and then spurious correlations are identified by testing for two other *a priori* assumptions.[23]

Based on this principle and on common-sense impressions, we can start off with parental background. If parents go to school before working to earn an income then their income can be a supposed effect of their schooling — not the other way round. Likewise, these two variables can affect the mass media exposure of children; again, not the other way, even if income level can probably have a stronger role than schooling. Access to mass media is probably a function of incomes, although schooling of parents probably improves it.

Then we can bring in community background. This variable

probably preceded parental background much further in time, although it can be brought close to the present by 'type of school'. These variables can be conceptually differentiated from each other. However, the data we have at the moment do not permit us to identify one from the other. And since the type of school is included in the analysis, it is likely that community background will recede as a statistically trivial variable.

All these correlates converge on measured general mental ability.[24] At the same time the possibility that mental ability may also influence the degree of mass media exposure is not negated. Although the causal direction between these variables is not easily defined, we consider mass media exposure influencing mental ability as the salient direction for analysis. None the less, if the analysis is carried forward, i.e. on to the connection between mass media exposure and test performance, the link would probably be indirect, i.e. through measured mental ability, so that the introduction of this variable would render a direct relationship trivial.

All told, the structural relationships of the variables would probably be as indicated in Figure 6.1.

Figure 6.1: Causal Chain of Correlates of Test Performance

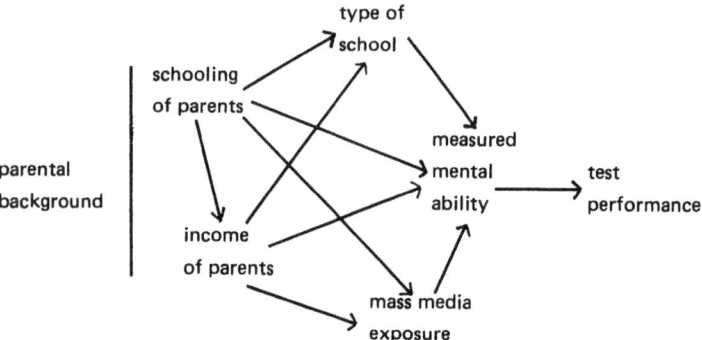

Parental background, a combination of the schooling and the income of parents, virtually defines the kind of schools the children go to and the kinds and quality of mass media they are exposed to, and these latter factors are the main determinants of differences in test performance. The type of school is certainly not the simple variable it may seem; it also defines what takes place in these schools, and the structure and quality of input resources to learning – the quality of teachers,

Educational Achievement in the Philippines

libraries, programmes, other school facilities, and even the raw material such as the pupils' willingness to learn. All this impinges on the measured general mental ability, which in turn bears on achievement test performance.

Access to the University of the Philippines

The University of the Philippines is interesting for our study because it caters only to a small and definitely non-representative group of the student population. In pursuit of excellence in its programmes it has also inexorably become elitist. It is proud to point out outstanding leaders of the country in whose education it has played a major part.

Every year the university administers an entrance examination to high school leavers who seek admission to it. On the basis of this examination, a decision is made whether or not a prospective student may be admitted. In 1975, only 25.65 per cent of those who applied passed the examination and were therefore qualified for admission.[25] What is at issue here is not how small or large this proportion is, but how representative that group is of the population.

At the moment we do not have full information for judging the representativeness (parity) of the group which qualifies for admission, but it is possible for us to seek indirect evidence from which inferences on parities or disparities can be made. Fortunately, there are published results of the examination, which can be reanalysed and presented simply.[26]

Data Analysis

In the published cross-tabulations of test results, with annual family income as a common column variable, a number of factors such as high school type, regional location, rural-urban location and type of secondary course were presented as row variables. This information presents an unusual opportunity to analyse somewhat rigorously the effect of the row and column variables on the probability of access to the university.[27]

Findings

By using the logarithms of incomes and the dummies of high school types as the independent variables to the logit probability of access or admission to the University of the Philippines, we show that income has a powerful influence on access, along with the type of high school previously attended by the student. High on the list are private schools, followed by public schools, including special public high schools. The figures (Table 6.16) show that the probability of access to the university is favourable to those graduating from these high schools but discriminates against those from barrio or village high schools and public vocational high schools.[28]

Table 6.16: Effect of High School Type and Family Income Origin on Probability of Admission to the University of the Philippines, 1975

Independent variables		Standardised regression coefficients
XVARO2 (In income)		0.62*
Dummies:	private school	0.72*
	general public school	0.46*
	special public school	0.24**
	barrio high school	−0.21*
	public vocational school	−0.26**
F = 45.87*	df = 6/61	Adj. R^2 = 0.77

*Significant at 1 per cent P level.
**Significant at 5 per cent P level.

Moving from the type of high schools, we focus attention on the type of programmes, namely academic, vocational and other programmes. Regression estimates reveal that graduating from an academic high school exerts a strong positive influence on the probability of passing the entrance examination, and hence on qualifying for admission. On the other hand, graduating from other high schools, including vocational schools, seems to have a negative effect, i.e. vocational school graduates stand much less chance of ever getting over the threshold of that university (see Table 6.17). Thus it is fairly clear that the University of the Philippines attracts students from high-income households, especially those graduating from academic private high schools. Obviously, it discourages, or discriminates against, students who do not possess this background.

Next, we look at regional disparities on access to the university. This can be inferred from the effect on probability of admission of the regional location of the high schools previously attended. Regression estimates of the influence of regional dummies (Table 6.18) seem to indicate that living close to the university or studying in high schools near the university, i.e. within the same region, has a favourable effect on the probability of admission. Students who attended high schools in regions 3 and 4 or in Central and Southern Luzon, respectively, tend to have a good chance of making it to the university, of which the two largest campuses happen to be located in region 4. Applicants from West Visayas seem to have less chances of admission than applicants from the first two regions just mentioned, and those coming from West Mindanao, East Visayas and other regions are quite unlikely to be admitted to the university.

Table 6.17: Effect of Type of Programme and Family Income Origin on Probability of Admission to the University of the Philippines, 1975

Independent variables		Standardised regression coefficients
XVARO2 (ln income)		0.52*
Dummies:	academic schools	0.55*
	other high schools	−0.53*
F = 77.89	df = 3/31	Adj. R^2 = 0.87

*Significant at 1 per cent P level.

Table 6.18: Effect of Regional Location of High School Graduated from and Family Income Origins on Probability of Admission to the University of the Philippines, 1975

Independent variables		Standardised regression coefficients
XVARO2 (ln income)		0.67*
Dummies:	Southern Luzon	0.64*
	Central Luzon	0.23*
	West Visayas	0.12*
	West Mindanao	−0.11*
	East Visayas	−0.09**
F = 84.88	df = 6/121	Adj. R^2 = 0.80

*Significant at 1 per cent P level.
**Significant at 5 per cent P level.

These data confirm previous suspicions that according to test results the university tends to attract students from within its immediate region and tends to reject prospective students from other regions, especially those from economically depressed areas such as West

100 *Educational Achievement in the Philippines*

Mindanao and East Visayas.[29]

This nearness bias in access or admission to the University of the Philippines is perhaps not really due to geographical proximity as such but partly to other factors, e.g. exposure to urbanisation. If this variable is regressed through dummies[30] along with the ln income[31] as independent variables on probability of admission, the impression emerges that students from high-income households who have studied at schools in metropolitan Manila stand a favourable chance of being admitted to the university. 'Other urban' as a dummy variable does not have a significant coefficient: if this dummy is substituted with 'rural' a negative coefficient is produced, which suggests that the effect of attending schools tends to be of trivial importance (in other urban areas) and even a negative factor when those schools are in rural areas. The figures in Table 6.19 clinch our argument that access (admission) to the university is heavily biased by high incomes and urban origin, especially from metropolitan Manila. But this is not saying that this bias is unique to the University of the Philippines. It is most probably true to any other academic institution which has achieved any quantum of excellence; in a broad sense, it merely highlights the disparities which cumulate since the prospective students were born.

Table 6.19: Effect of Urban Location of High School and Family Income Origin on the Probability of Admission to the University of the Philippines

Independent variables	Standardised regression coefficients
XVAR02 (ln income)	0.85*
Dummies: metropolitan Manila	0.37*
other urban	0.11

F = 65.63	df = 3/38	Adj. R^2 = 0.83

*Significant at 1 per cent P level.

Admission, however, is only the beginning. There is no telling about what happens after that event, especially the systematic effects of certain factors on graduation and eventual employment. General impressions suggest that schooling tends to strengthen even more the already heavy bias towards students coming from high-income urban households.

Summary

Our analysis of educational achievement in the Philippines began by stressing one positive factor. On the basis of sex grouping, educational deprivation of females — a prominent feature in many Asian countries — seems almost non-existent there.

On a regional basis, wide disparities are evident. What is somewhat disturbing, although not surprising, is that these disparities seem associated with regional development levels. Children from low-income regions not only have poor attendance rates but also have low scores in scholastic achievement tests.

Other elements in our analysis are more discouraging. The limiting effects of poor home background (schooling and income level of parents), rural background, type of school attended and other factors on scholastic activities or on learning outcomes which were observed during the final year of secondary schooling are not peculiar to the secondary level. Our analysis of data published under Project SOUTELE shows that the same factors appear to be operative at the elementary school level, and by backward extrapolation, the same factors may have their grip even before the children set foot in schools, tightening their hold on the children's future as schooling progresses. Those who do not have the means nor the gift of early display of talent drop out.

The case of admissions to the University of the Philippines, a tax-supported institution, strengthens this view. On the basis of examination results, the probability of access to the university is highly biased toward the high-income groups. The evidence reveals that this institution is almost a preserve of rich students coming from metropolitan Manila and other urban areas.

Several variables were found to have a significant influence on scholastic achievement, namely (a) educational level of the population, (b) income level of households (in geographical units of analysis), (c) distribution (or spread) of the educational level, and (d) regional variables. The last of these seems to reflect the level of development of the region or province. There are indications that these variables interplay with each other. For example, (a) and (b) above appear complementary in promoting achievement; when one is at a somewhat low level, the other seems more important.

The impression is that access to schools and further schooling (and on to high-income occupations) is largely dependent on the income level of parents. While an early display of talent and assiduity may to some extent be a substitute for high parental income, the limiting effects of low incomes of households on scholastic achievement of children and their access to more schooling are formidable. This evidence gives us a clue to the intergenerational reproduction of inequality which, without appropriate public intervention, would be likely to continue to worsen even when schools are expanded ostensible to serve the poor.

Appendix

Description of the NCEE, 1973 (Excerpts from FAPE, *EDB Statistical Bulletin*, Vol. 1, No. 2, October 1974)

The 1973 NCEE provides a set of four scores in the Mental Ability section and three scores in the Subject Proficiency section. The four subtests comprising the Mental Ability section are as follows:

1. Abstract Reasoning (AR) measures the ability to recognise or comprehend figural changes involving visual information. Each item of the AR subtest is made up of five figures all of which are enclosed in uniform-sized squares. The task of the examinee is to identify which does not exhibit the information that enables one to transform one figure into another within the given set of figures.
2. Verbal Analogies (VA) measures the ability to recognise or comprehend semantic items of information. Each item of this subtest consists of five pairs of words. The task of the examinee is to recognise the relationship between the first pair and then identify which among the other four pairs follow the same relationship.
3. Number and Letter Series (NLS) measures the ability to recognise or comprehend the structure or organisation of a system of symbolic information. Each item in this subtest is made up of a stem consisting of a series of numbers or letters of the English alphabet and a set of four options which are numbers or letters as the case may be. The examinee's task is to discover the rule involved in the development of the given series of symbols and to give an objective record of his cognition by picking from the four given options the symbol that should follow the last symbol in the given series.

4. Word-Number Relations (WNR) measures the ability to memorise relations between symbolic forms of information. Each item is made up of a stem consisting of two word-number pairs plus an unmatched word and a set of options made up of a string of numbers. The task of the examinee is to identify the rule by which each of the first two given pairs are related and to keep this in memory in searching for the proper match of the given word in the stem from among the given options.

The Subject Proficiency section of the NCEE consists of subject matter tests in English, Mathematics and Science. The component items for each of these subtests are:

1. English (Eng) – grammar and usage, sentence structure, ordering of sentence parts, word meaning and reading comprehension.
2. Mathematics (Math) – geometry and measurement, algebra, arithmetic and others.
3. Science (Sc) – biology, chemistry and physics.

Scoring

Not all of the scores in the seven subtests are reported. For a more reliable prediction of the scholastic performance, VA, NLS and WNR scores were combined into a single score called the Symbolic and Verbal Relations (SVR) score. The scores in the rest of the subtests are reported as separate scores.

The overall score represented by the General Scholastic Aptitude (GSA) score is the simple average of the five scores in AR, SVR, Eng, Math and Sc. The GSA summarises in a single measure the complex intellectual trait being tapped by the test. The GSA formula may be expressed symbolically as follows:

$$GSA = \frac{1}{5} [AR + Eng + Math + Sc + \frac{1}{3} (VA + NLS + WNR)]$$

The scores are reported in standard or scaled form using a common scale with a range of 200 to 800. The scaling procedure simply involved transforming each of the subtest raw-score distribution into a distribution that has a mean of 500 and a standard deviation of 100. When the standard scale is established, we have for every raw score of the test a corresponding value on the standard scale.

The statistical index attached to the NCEE scores is represented by the percentile rank. For a given subtest, the percentile rank of a given NCEE score gives the percentage of the total number of examinees who obtained scores below the given score.

Characteristics of SOUTELE Tests

Table 6A.1: Validity Coefficients of the Achievement Test for Grade VI

Tests	:	r	:	SE_r
Reading		.3804 (.38)		.0056
Language		.4113 (.41)		.0054
Pagbasa		.3739 (.37)		.0057
Wika		.3954 (.40)		.0055
Mathematics		.3410 (.34)		.0058
Science		.4030 (.40)		.0055
Social Studies		.3672 (.37)		.0057
Work Education (Boys)		.2924 (.29)		.006
Home Economics (Girls)		.4336 (.43)		.0054

Source: SOUTELE, Vol. 1, Table 2, p.31.

As shown above, the obtained correlation values, also known as validity coefficients, range from .29 for Work Education to .43 for Home Economics. Considering the possible unreliability of the teachers' ratings due to the recent adoption of a new rating system in the elementary grades, the obtained validity coefficients may be considered high enough for purposes of this study.

Table 6A.2: Reliability Coefficients and Standard Errors of Measurement of the Achievement Tests for Grade VI

Tests	No. of items	No. of pupils tested	M	SD	r_{tt}	SE_{meas}
Reading (English)	40	23,099	16.05	7.24	.84	2.90
Language (English)	70	23,100	27.91	9.71	.83	4.00
Pagbasa	50	23,093	22.71	9.54	.88	3.30
Wika	60	23,092	30.61	11.24	.896	3.60
Elem. Math.	40	23,089	14.46	5.48	.71	2.955
Elem. Science	50	23,092	24.07	8.91	.86	3.30
Social Studies	30	23,092	14.42	5.37	.76	2.631
Work Education	30	11,051	12.68	3.99	.56	2.633
Home Economics	30	12,037	14.47	5.00	.72	2.645

*Calculations of the r_{tt} were based on Kuder-Richardson Formula No. 21.
Source: SOUTELE, Vol. 1, Table 3, p. 32.

Table 6A.3: Reliability Coefficients and Other Related Data on the Non-verbal Mental Ability Tests (Final Form) Administered to Grade VI Pupils (N = 23,151)

Subtest	No. of items		pq	r_{tt}	SE_{meas}
I. Association	10	2.10	4.41	2.203	.501	1.484
II. A Classification	10	2.15	4.6225	2.049	.558	1.432
B Classification	10	2.77	7.6729	2.161	.718	1.470
C Classification	10	2.09	4.3681	2.170	.503	1.473
III. Analogy	10	2.59	6.7081	2.419	.640	1.555
IV. Visual Acuity	10	2.43	5.9049	2.325	.607	1.525
V. Spatial Relationships	10	2.12	4.4944	1.323	.706	1.150
VI. A Abstract Reasoning	10	2.79	7.7841	2.249	.712	1.500
B Abstract Reasoning	20	3.35	11.2225	4.401	.609	2.098
TOTAL	100	14.28	203.9184	21.300	.900	4.512

Source: SOUTELE, Vol. 1, Table 12, p. 59.

Table 6A.4: Mean Scores of Grade VI Pupils on the Non-verbal Mental Ability Tests (Final Form)

Subtests	No. of items	Mean	SD
I. Association	10	6.08	2.10
II. A Classification	10	5.68	2.15
B Classification	10	5.99	2.77
C Classification	10	4.95	2.09
III. Analogy	10	4.52	2.59
IV. Visual Acuity	10	4.34	.243
V. Spatial Relationships	10	8.32	2.12
VI. A Abstract Reasoning	10	5.10	2.79
B Abstract Reasoning	20	8.10	3.35
TOTAL	100		

Source: SOUTELE, Vol. 1, Table 13, p. 60.

Notes

1. For details on the NCEE and for characteristics of the SOUTELE tests see Appendix.

2. Presidential Commission to Survey Philippine Education, *Education for National Development* (Manila, 1970).

3. Literacy was defined for the purposes of the 1970 Philippine census as ability to read and write a simple message in some language or dialect.

4. The differences in attendance rates are divided by their corresponding base figures and the quotients are expressed in per cent by simply multiplying them by 100. The rural-urban difference in attendance rates of 6.5, for example, is equivalent to a gap of 25.04 per cent.

5. The provinces can also be divided into rural and urban areas as defined for the purposes of the 1970 Philippine census.

6. In this sense, access is defined very narrowly, i.e. in terms of attendance.

7. In 1973 the cut-off was 25 percentile score; a score below this cut-off is a disqualification. See Appendix for details of the NCEE.

8. This statement does not presuppose that any difference is inherently due to sex but to factors which are associated with sex, e.g. cultural factors, and probably also to career opportunities.

9. Recall the results of Byron W. Brown and Daniel H. Saks in 'The Production and Distribution of Cognitive Skills Within Schools', *Journal of Political Economy*, Vol. 83 (June 1975), and also those of the IEA studies. However, test results in Manila varied more than those in the provinces. This is in contrast to what was found in the IEA studies that results varied more in the three less developed countries than in the advanced countries. The greater variability found among the three less developed countries could be due to the IEA test

itself, which may have been less reliable at low levels of ability.

10. We need another data set for a different time period in order to detect any levelling up of test scores.

11. The test data analysed in this section are the results of the 1973 NCEE published by the Fund for Assistance to Private Education (FAPE) in a series of R and D Reports. For a technical description of the test, see Appendix.

12. We would hasten to add that even if the coefficient of household income failed to reach a statistically significant level, its sign is negative. It seems to show that high household income level tends to reduce the spread of the scores away from the mean.

13. As may be shown by a high correlation between literacy and income.

14. The subjects are: reading, language (English), pagbasa (reading in Filipino), mathematics, science, social studies and work education. The last subject consists of gardening and shopwork for boys and home economics for girls. See Appendix for details of the test characteristics.

15. *Survey of Outcomes of Elementary Education*, SOUTELE (Manila, The Department of Education and Culture, May 1976). This is a two-volume work consisting of a Technical Report (Vol. 1) and another report (Vol. 2) for a general audience.

16. There are a few peculiarities which need to be explained. We need to test the statistical significance of the differences in test scores of Grade V children from different types of schools. But this step awaits new data. Setting the results in Grade VI aside, we can offer only hunches on the observed differences (in test scores). The rather simple expectation that pupils in private schools come from high-income groups, i.e. are exposed to a more favourable home environment in terms of educational resources and therefore ought to be doing better than children in central schools, appears not to be justified. A plausible explanation is that these differences reflect patterns of emphasis: perhaps central schools lay more importance on the national language (i.e in pagbasa and wika), practical subjects (i.e. work education and home economics) and social studies than do private schools, while the latter concentrate on science and English language. But this hunch leaves several unanswered questions,e.g. concerning test score differences in mathematics, especially between village schools and private schools, and also in science in Grade VI. Another explanation seems to be needed.

17. We have to remind the reader that the analysis is cross-sectional as an approximation of an evolutionary, longitudinal change in test performance.

18. There is a plausible explanation for this observation; but pending its verification we can only pose it as a hypothesis: namely that children in the different types of schools have different learning curves and, correspondingly, that children (as they are affected by different factors) could be at different stages of their learning curves. Thus, stimulated by better home background and probably by better schools, children in private schools were at a stage where learning speed was accelerating at an increasing rate whereas children in barrio schools could still be in the early, fast stage of their curves.

19. See Appendix.

20. Some remarks have to be made, however, on the figures on listening to radio and watching television. It seems to us that pupils in barrio schools and central schools have more or less similar access to radio but not to television. Furthermore, pupils in private schools appear to watch television more than listen to radio; this probably explains the low figures for this group of pupils *vis-à-vis* the other groups in regard to radio.

21. Technical Report, Project SOUTELE, p. 304.

22. See Jae-On Kim and F.J. Kohout, 'Special Topics in General Linear

Models' in Norman H. Nie *et al., Statistical Package for the Social Sciences*, 2nd edn (New York, McGraw Hill, 1970); also M.D. Leonor Jr, *Education and Productivity: Some Evidence and Implications* (Geneva, ILO, 1976).

23. Namely (a) that certain variables are not directly dependent on certain others, i.e. that the observed correlation does not disappear when another variable is introduced, and (b) that the error terms, in a set of recursive equations, are uncorrelated. See Herbert A. Simon, 'Spurious Correlation: A Causal Interpretation' in H.M. Blalock Jr (ed.), *Causal Models in the Social Sciences* (Chicago, Aldine Atherton, 1971), pp. 5-17. Simon remarks: 'correlation is proof of causation in [a] two-variable case if . . . the assumptions of time precedence and non-correlation of . . . error terms [are valid]'.

24. We stress here that measured general mental ability is different from the abstract concept of intelligence: 'measurement' readily calls to mind the bias of the measuring stick, i.e. the tests, and of the sample of abilities being tested.

25. See Dr Romeo L. Manlapaz, 'Democratization of the University Admissions Policy' in *U.P. Newsletter*, Vol. LV, No. 36 (September 1976), pp. 3ff.

26. We draw heavily on data published by Manlapaz, ibid.

27. Symbolically, this is written:

P_{ij} = proportion of qualified examinees (n_{ij}) in the ith, j^{th} cell in relation to total (N) admissions.

I_j = midpoint of the income at the jth income column; those of the lower and upper tails are approximations.

D_i = row dummies.

After a logit transformation of P_{ij}, the following function was estimated:

$L_{ij} = f(I_j, D_i)$,
where $L_{ij} = \ln(P_{ij}/(1-P_{ij}))$,
and L_j's were in natural logarithms.

The logit transformation was used to tidy up the P_{ij}, i.e. to remove the lower and upper boundaries (see Henri Theil, *Statistical Decomposition Analysis* (Amsterdam, North Holland Publishing Company, 1973), Ch. 4). The midpoints of the lowest and highest income intervals are approximated by 2/3 and 5/3 of the upper and lower bounds respectively (see Farhad Mehran, *Dealing with Grouped Income Distribution Data* mimeographed World Employment Programme research working paper No. 20 (2-23)(restricted) (Geneva, ILO, 1975), pp. 11-12.

28. This typology is based on source of support. Private high schools are financed largely from non-governmental funds, i.e. either as proprietary institutions or as schools run by religious orders and foundations. All public high schools, however, are tax supported. But they differ in other respects. A general public high school offers a general education curriculum while a special public high school may have a science bias or other special instruction in its programmes. A public vocational school differs from the rest in that it specialises in vocational training. A barrio high school is like a general high school; its curriculum is general and it is a public school, too, legally speaking. In reality, however, its support is mainly from pupils' fees. As its name indicates it is usually located in a small village and it utilises the facilities and teachers of an elementary school there.

29. The gross regional products of Southern Luzon and Central Luzon amount to 46.89 and 7.36 per cent respectively of the gross national product; the corresponding figures for West Mindanao and East Visayas are 2.82 and 3.07 per cent. (B. Prantilla (ed.), 'Regional Development and Planning: The Philippine Experience' in *Proceedings of a Seminar on Industrialisation Strategies and the*

Growth Pole Approach to Regional Planning and Development, Nagoya, Japan, 4-13 November 1975 (Nagoya, UNCRD, 1976), citing NEDA Regional Account Project, 1974.)

30. The dummies can be arranged according to a descending gradient, e.g. metropolitan Manila, other urban and rural location schools. This gradient can be used as a proxy to degree of exposure to urbanisation.

31. 'ln income' means the logarithm of income. The use of ln income follows from the observation that the frequency distribution of income is usually log-normal, i.e. bell-shaped, when income is transformed to its logarithm.

7 SCHOOL ENROLMENT IN INDIA, SRI LANKA AND THAILAND

The previous chapter discussed the influence which household background factors are likely to have on children's success in developing their abilities in school. For other countries we do not have the same detailed information, particularly on the development of tested ability, as we have for the Philippines. Nevertheless, we can make use of a variety of sources to build up a series of very similar pictures. Unlike the Philippines, many other countries show the effects of household factors on school achievement at a very basic level, that of enrolment in primary schools. Effects on school enrolment at higher levels and on the development of mental abilities are, of course, also prominent. Nevertheless, many Asian countries are still at a stage of persuading parents and children of the value of education and finding differences in the response of various groups.

To these differences there are classic responses, including compulsory schooling, equalisation of levels of teacher training, measures to enlist parental support for education or the provision of free meals and other inducements and free school textbooks; but even all these measures are unlikely to secure high enrolment rates, uniform for all social groups, after the mid-teens, and even for earlier years they are not likely to eliminate the influence of parental encouragement. In the poorer developing countries a start is usually only just being made on the introduction of measures of this type which are naturally restricted by the availability of government funds. It is to the simplest of these issues that we will first turn, i.e. to factors influencing school attendance and school enrolment. First, we discuss primary education in India (with a brief mention of Bangladesh), and then school attendance and enrolment in Sri Lanka. After a brief discussion of Thailand we conclude by discussing some of the major influences behind educational policy-making in Asia in recent years.

Primary Education in India

One common representation of the role of primary education in India is that it is the much sought-after avenue for social advance, and is

School Enrolment in India, Sri Lanka and Thailand 111

desired for their children's sake by parents in all sections of society: in Mandelbaum's words, 'modern education has become a prime source of both prestigious symbols and substantive power, so most aspiring groups put heavy emphasis on the education of their children'.[1] He gives example after example of the support given for expanded education by caste associations, by Jats in Meerut, by Telis (merchants and oil-seed crushers) in Orissa and by potters in Uttar Pradesh. These groups not only pass resolutions at their meetings but also take positive steps to establish schools, hostels and scholarships.

Such apparent enthusiasm for education is backed up by other surveys. For example, the National Council of Educational Research and Training, in an inquiry into the needs of tribal people, found only 4 per cent of parents unwilling to educate their children.[2] Furthermore, while 29 per cent of parents considered that the extent of their children's schooling depended on the child, another 44 per cent wished to see their children at least as graduates; 93 per cent of families were anxious to educate their daughters. The general motive for the widespread enthusiasm for education was to achieve a higher standard of living for the family as a whole. However, this picture of anxious parents only waiting for the government to provide educational facilities is somewhat marred by the negative response of some 20 per cent of parents to another question, asking whether they could afford to send their children to primary schools. In this particular inquiry all the villages surveyed were served by primary schools not more than three miles off. In a further survey undertaken by Professor Barnabas[3] 95 per cent of sampled parents stated their wish that their children should receive more education than they themselves had received, and 83 per cent specifically considered that girls should be educated. Moreover, while in both these surveys the first reason given for educating children in general was economic, the first reason for educating girls was more personal — that the daughters should be wiser or live better in some other sense.

A more pessimistic, and in many ways, one suspects, more realistic, picture was presented by A.R. Desai[4] in a survey of 153 families in a slum area in Bombay. It was found that only 60 per cent of children (70 per cent of boys and 46 per cent of girls) in the 6-14 age group were attending school. The author of the survey gives three major reasons for non-attendance: poverty, i.e. the need for children to make some contribution, however indirect, to the running of the household; lack of interest on the part of the children; and, correspondingly, lack of interest on the part of the parents. No doubt these points interact.

Nevertheless, in reply to other questions the majority of parents said they wished to educate their sons at least up to matriculation standard and their daughters up to middle school level. It was clear in the survey that in many cases parents' aspirations for their children's education and future occupation were totally unrealistic and that high hopes were still held for children who had already dropped out of school. Nevertheless, it was clear that many aspirations were intensely held. In this survey, as in others, the main reason given for educating boys was 'to get a good job'. This reason was also given for daughters' education, but to a much lesser extent — and predominantly by those who wanted their daughter at least to matriculate; most parents envisaged a relatively low level of education as 'sufficient'.

Before passing on to a few harder facts on enrolment and dropout in Indian primary education, it is necessary to mention the caste issue which is, after all, a major concern in South Asia. Although caste ranking can be changed and the exact position of many caste groups is unclear, it is fairly obvious who is at the top and the bottom. Caste status, particularly at the bottom end of the scale, is strongly correlated with income, but low caste will have its own effects on aspirations, all the more so because successful education is by no means sufficient to give social acceptability to someone of low-caste origins. As Scarlett Epstein[5] has it, 'social pressures operate through the medium of the family and marital relationships and thereby perpetuate social differentiation in urban societies in spite of higher education'. In the villages the position is socially more conservative.

The strong connection between low caste and low income can be illustrated from some survey data from Central India showing the occupations of members of 'backward and scheduled castes', to use the official terminology. The data for rural areas are not so satisfactory since the description 'cultivator' will cover a wide range of landholding and operating size groups. (Data are available on the distribution of landholdings overall and among scheduled caste households in Maharashtra, for 1961: overall, 37 per cent of households cultivated under two hectares, compared to 47 per cent of scheduled caste households; 28 per cent of households overall cultivated over six hectares, compared to 18 per cent of scheduled caste households.) In fact, it is the polarisation of occupational categories within these groups in urban areas which is the most striking.

Caste would appear strongly to affect the desire for girls' education. In Barnabas's[6] sample, the share of parents unwilling to educate their daughters rises from 6 per cent in his 'high caste' group of respondents,

Table 7.1: Caste and Occupation (per cent)

Rural	Brahmans and other high castes	Backward and scheduled castes	Total
Cultivator	41.2	19.4	33.4
Professional	14.4	2.4	4.4
Managerial	4.4	5.7	3.5
Commercial	22.3	6.4	6.3
Semi-skilled	3.3	34.2	25.9
Unskilled	14.4	31.9	26.5
Total	100.0	100.0	100.0
Urban			
Cultivator	2.7	2.2	1.9
Professional	22.2	3.3	8.1
Managerial	12.4	2.2	7.8
Commercial	43.5	13.0	27.2
Semi-skilled	6.8	51.6	29.3
Unskilled	12.4	27.7	25.7
Total	100.0	100.0	100.0

Source: E.D. Driver, 'Caste and Occupational Structure in Central India', *Social Forces*, Vol. XLI (1962).

to 36 per cent in his 'lowest caste' group. Desai[7] cites the point that since education for boys is so frequently seen as an avenue to good job opportunities, and since girls are not generally expected to work outside the house, education for girls would be irrational. Adams[8] quotes further data from Driver[9] to show that years of education received customarily fall with the social standing of the caste. In a survey of employed persons 68 per cent of rural and 87 per cent of urban Brahmans had received more than a primary education, while only 6 per cent of rural and 17 per cent of urban scheduled castes had done so. These are, of course, the results which would be expected from the occupational distribution of these groups shown in Table 7.1.

It is remarkably difficult to find, for India, data which can link enrolment and use of educational facilities to household variables, particularly income or consumption. Some information, however, can be gleaned from the field work of the Agricultural Economics Research Centre in Delhi.[10] In a 1967 survey of over 2,000 families in eleven villages in Uttar Pradesh and nine in the Punjab they recorded school enrolment rates (ages 6-7) for two income groups and for two caste groups: Harijan (previously 'Untouchable') and others. Their sample families were grouped as follows:

114 *School Enrolment in India, Sri Lanka and Thailand*

Family Income	Harijan	Non-Harijan	Total Sample
Under Rs 1,500 p.a.	74	56	64
Over Rs 1,500 p.a.	26	44	36
	100	100	100

The enrolment rates were as follows:

Income		Harijan	Non-Harijan
(i) below Rs 1,500 p.a.	(ii) above Rs 1,500 p.a.		
26.1	47.3	27.8	39.1

In this example it can be calculated that caste does appear to have an independent effect on enrolment. If only the family income bracket were a determining factor the percentage enrolment figures for Harijans and non-Harijans would have a spread of only some 4 percentage points instead of 11.[11]

An extensive survey, using much more precise income categories, was made in West Bengal, a state which in educational terms ranks above the national average, but not by very much. These data, collected by Maitra, Day and Bhattarcharya,[12] are given in Table 7.2.

Table 7.2: West Bengal: Enrolment and Retention Rates (per cent)

	Rural						Urban					
	Males			Females			Males			Females		
Quintile group*	I	II	II/I	I	II	II/I	I	II	II/I	I	II	II/I
0- 20	37	17	46	16	9	56	45	19	42	29	24	83
20- 40	48	28	58	19	—	—	46	33	72	52	35	67
40- 60	57	30	53	24	—	—	64	57	89	72	67	93
60- 80	62	60	97	31	20	64	84	82	98	81	43	53
80-100	72	47	65	57	48	84	86	72	84	85	70	82

*Ranged in ascending order of *per capita* expenditure.
I = age group 6-14; II = age group 15-17; II/I = the ratio of the enrolment rates of the two age groups.
Source: T. Maitra *et al., An Enquiry into the Distribution of Public Education and Health Services in West Bengal.*

The data in Table 7.2 relate not to primary education as such but to enrolment rates for two different age groups. It is quite possible that even the older age group is still in primary education. Looking first at the enrolment rates for the younger age groups, it is seen that in all cases they rise steadily with income level: obviously income has an important influence on enrolment rates. However, the data for the younger age group are quite compatible with a high initial enrolment rate, at the age of 6 or 7, for children of all income groups, but far higher drop-out rates for the poorer groups. Presumably the actual situation lies somewhere between the two. To make rural-urban comparisons from these data it is best, as a simple rule of thumb, to compare any rural income group with the next higher urban group in order to take account of the higher average income in urban areas; i.e. one should make the comparisons upwards from left to right. In this way the results for younger boys are very similar, as indeed are those for older boys with the exception of the richest rural quintile. For girls the position is reversed; rural rates are consistently below urban rates, often considerably so, with again the exception of the richer rural quintile whose enrolment rate for older girls of 48 per cent exceeds the corresponding urban rate of 43 per cent.

Comparisons of the enrolment of girls and boys show generally higher rates for males in rural areas for both age groups, with the exception of the richest quintile. In urban areas the rates are broadly similar except in the poorest quintile for the younger group. Retention rates (here the enrolment rate of the older age group divided by that of the younger) do not vary much between urban and rural areas, for boys. For girls there are some obvious and considerable differences except in the top two quintiles. Both rural-urban residence and relative incomes would appear to affect the education enrolment of boys and girls separately.

Some very interesting information on the causes of school drop-out can be taken from another study of the National Council of Educational Research and Training.[13] This was a study of some 1,200 pupils and ex-pupils, of whom some 40 per cent were in school, covering Grades I-VIII. The sampled schools were taken from Maharashtra, Punjab, Rajasthan, Delhi and Himachal Pradesh. Annual rates of drop-out in the sample were generally highest at Grade I, where they varied from 7 to 17 per cent. For most years the rates were of the order of 6-10 per cent. The study concluded: 'Such variables as the qualifications of teachers, the per capita income of teachers and the distance of teachers' residence from school do have some relationship with the rate of drop-out, though the relationship is very weak.'[14]

Turning to pupil and to household variables, the report presented a large number of variables cross-classified by 'stay-in' or 'drop-out'. The most interesting of these are presented in Table 7.3. A problem here is that the drop-outs in question occurred in any of eight grades, so that different factors may very well be important in determining the drop-out rate at each grade. However, where the survey report ranks reasons for drop-out separately for elementary, primary and middle schools, the ranking shows very little variation. Certain variables, of which by far the most important is regularity of attendance at school, appear to predominate in all examples. This can be demonstrated from the data in Table 7.3. If each percentage of stay-ins and drop-outs is divided by the average the resulting figure gives the degree of departure from the average. If all these differences from the average are summed, irrespective of sign, and divided by the number of observations, a ranking of the importance of the variables in explaining drop-outs results. In this example, the overall ranking was found to be as follows:

(a) regularity of attendance;
(b) home motivation (measured by 'relevance to education of activities for which pupils perceived they were rewarded by their parents');
(c) age of admission to Grade I;
(d) caste;
(e) household income.

Income is, therefore, far from being the most important explanatory variable. In the highest income class, 46 per cent of children, admittedly a lower percentage than in other classes, had dropped out. How far irregular attendance is related to income class cannot be shown from the data. It is quite possible that most of those with poor attendance records were from low-income families; but in that case quite a number of children from relatively high-income families, with a good attendance record, who had possibly begun their education at the prescribed age, also dropped out. Home motivation, presumably, largely determines both attendance and age of admission, so that the predominant reason for dropping out is apparently of that kind. Again, many low-income families, if not most, may fall into the 'low motivation' category. However, low income is clearly not the only cause of low motivation.

As is well known, the government of India has taken seriously

Table 7.3: Drop-outs and Other Variables (per cent)

(a) Regularity of attendance

	(I) −60%	(II) 60−80%	(III) 80%+	(IV) Average	(I)/(IV)	(III)/(IV)
Drop-outs	100	87	36	63	1.66	0.57
Stay-ins	—	13	64	37	0	1.73

(b) Home motivation: rewards for activities

	Irrelevant	Neutral	Relevant	Average	(I)/(IV)	(III)/(IV)
Drop-outs	74	75	35	58	1.27	0.60
Stay-ins	26	25	65	42	0.62	1.55

(c) Age at admission to Grade I

	−6	7−8	9+	Average	(I)/(IV)	(III)/(IV)
Drop-outs	41	65	87	58	0.71	1.50
Stay-ins	59	35	13	42	1.40	0.31

(d) Caste

	(I) Scheduled	(II) Backward	(III) Kshatriya	(IV) Vaisya	(V) Brahmin	(VI) Average	(I)/(VI)	(II)/(VI)	(III)/(VI)	(IV)/(VI)	(V)/(VI)
Drop-outs	76	77	52	34	50	61	1.24	1.26	0.85	0.56	0.82
Stay-ins	24	23	48	66	50	39	0.61	0.59	1.23	1.69	1.28

(e) Family income Rs p.a.

	(I) −1000	(II) 1001−1500	(III) 1501−2000	(IV) 2001−3000	(V) 3001+	(VI) Average	(I)/(VI)	(II)/(VI)	(III)/(VI)	(IV)/(VI)	(VI)/(VI)
Drop-outs	72	68	64	61	46	62	1.16	1.11	1.03	0.98	0.74
Stay-ins	28	32	36	39	54	38	0.74	0.84	0.95	1.03	1.92

Source: National Council of Educational Research and Training, *Wastage and Stagnation in Primary and Middle Schools* (Delhi, 1968).

the issue of the social and economic uplift of members of scheduled castes and scheduled tribes. Overall, the former account for some 15 per cent and the latter some 7 per cent of the total population. Scheduled tribes, however, are more concentrated geographically and some 75 per cent are found in the six states of Rajasthan, Orissa, Bihar, Madhya Pradesh, Assam and Gujarat. Scheduled tribes cannot be fitted into the caste hierarchy although they are generally looked down on by caste people. However, in 1961 some 68 per cent of the scheduled tribe labour force were cultivators (compared to 37 per cent of the scheduled caste workers) and some 20 per cent were agricultural labourers (compared to 34 per cent of the scheduled castes). Mandelbaum tells indeed of Bhils, who are often economically very underprivileged, being accepted by the Gujarat Rajput caste association.[15]

The Indian Constitution, Article 46, calls on the state to 'promote with special care the educational and economic interests of the weaker sections of the people, and, in particular of the scheduled castes and scheduled tribes'. This has been done in various ways; areas where scheduled tribes predominate are subject to special legislation on land alienation and restitution and on debt redemption. However, the best-known programmes in support of these groups relate to education and the organised labour market. Such programmes include job reservation in government and in public corporations and enterprises, scholarships, hostels and other facilities for students, place reservation in technical institutes and universities, and lower entrance qualifications for certain courses. The purpose of these schemes is to assist in escape from a deprived home background through upward social mobility.

It is fair to say that most of these provisions are demand oriented, that is their effect is to stimulate families towards relying on education or towards making necessary sacrifices at certain stages in the children's education in order to reap more likely benefits later. Efforts are also made on the supply side, through e.g. the provision of residential (ashram) schools in lightly populated tribal areas, or the training of teachers in tribal languages. However, for the scheduled castes at least, the supply of educational facilities is the same as for the poorer population as a whole. For primary education this is likely to mean that while the overall level of coverage may be fair, schools are likely to be located on sites more favourable to the access of the higher caste groups.

As a result of the stress on upward mobility in the special programmes for these groups the share of resources devoted to primary education scholarships, stipends, book grants etc. is low. The Report of the Education Commission[16] shows that in the early 1960s only 8 per

School Enrolment in India, Sri Lanka and Thailand

cent of scholarships and stipends were awarded for primary education. In the State of Maharashtra such expenditure on all pre-matriculation courses was only 20 per cent of the total.[17] Maharashtra is, however, a special case since, as Table 7.4 shows, the enrolment of scheduled caste children is very high. However, a point which is clearly made by Suma Chitnis[18] is that, even in Maharasthra, scheduled caste school enrolment varies inversely with the concentration of scheduled caste people in any area. This may be because a larger concentration of scheduled caste people is an indication of their greater poverty in certain areas, or because there are mutually reinforcing doubts about the appropriateness and desirability of education.

Table 7.4: Primary School Enrolment Rates, Selected States*

State	General	Scheduled castes	Scheduled tribes
Andra Pradesh	71.4	72.4	n.a.
Bihar	64.6	47.6	44.6
Gujarat	88.4	101.8	n.a.
Madhya Pradesh	56.5	42.7	n.a.
Maharashtra	90.0	167.2	n.a.
Mysore	88.6	84.6	n.a.
Orissa	67.0	66.0	47.9
Punjab	68.5	45.3	n.a.
Rajasthan	59.9	44.5	32.1
Uttar Pradesh	85.4	54.3	n.a.
West Bengal	72.2	59.5	n.a.

*These data are of school enrolments for Grades I-V as a percentage of the population aged 6-11. Obviously these two populations may not correspond, and enrolment rates of over 100 per cent are therefore quite possible. In addition, the data for scheduled castes and scheduled tribes assume that these groups have the same demographic structure as the general population. In fact they are likely to be younger than the average, in which case their enrolment rate shown above is exaggerated.
Sources: UNICEF, *Statistical Profile of Children and Youth in India* (Delhi, 1972) and *Report of the Commissioner for Scheduled Castes and Scheduled Tribes, 1971-2 and 1972-3* (Delhi, 1974).

In addition to specific grants to primary students, it is also general policy that education for scheduled caste and scheduled tribe pupils in government schools should be free of tuition and examination fees. In fact, the Education Commission Report shows that in any event less than 10 per cent of pupils in primary education were paying tuition fees. Various direct private costs, above all for books, are often more important than fees. The State of Bihar, for example, was during the 1960s providing average book grants of 50 rupees a year, but to only

4,000 pupils. By 1971 some 11,000 pupils were receiving book grants and some 16,000 primary and middle school pupils received stipends.[19] Other forms of assistance include a scheme in Maharashtra for the award of Rs 10 per annum to the two most competent scheduled caste pupils in Grades I-IV.[20] In all, in the late 1960s Maharashtra was assisting between 120,000 and 150,000 pupils at an average rate of Rs 20-25 per annum. Different states have received varying degrees of praise or accusation for their support, or lack of it, for such educational programmes from the Commissioner for Scheduled Castes and Scheduled Tribes. Thus Madhya Pradesh gives a 'substantial quantum of assistance', while in Rajasthan 'the coverage of assistance is extremely low, with the result that a large number of Scheduled Caste and Scheduled Tribe students go without any assistance whatsoever'.[21]

Although clearly schemes for financial assistance in primary education have a very limited coverage — for example, in Bihar in the 1960s they covered less than 10 per cent of tribal pupils[22] — their efficiency is firmly believed in. The Education Commission recommended that 5 per cent of all students (not just scheduled caste and scheduled tribe students) should be receiving scholarships by 1986. From his report, it would appear that the Commissioner for Scheduled Castes and Scheduled Tribes is firmly convinced that extended assistance programmes would promote higher enrolment rates. These authorities often see such assistance schemes as means of persuading the families of academically successful children to stay on into secondary and higher education; their role in ensuring a complete primary education for all is usually subordinated to that of selecting and favouring the meritorious.

A study of some 660 tribal students receiving financial assistance[23] sheds some light on the efficiency of financial assistance in encouraging enrolment. Although 55 per cent reported the assistance they received as 'inadequate', 45 per cent could still continue even unassisted. However, the report states that of the 660 students, 134 had dropped out at one stage or another but 'later on, within a year or two, these students again joined schools when financial assistance was provided'.[24] The assistance programmes, however, obviously suffer from some common disadvantages experienced by similar programmes in India: selection of beneficiaries devolves on a committee which often meets irregularly, and funds are frequently disbursed late. Such delay is quite likely to lead to absenteeism and to a misuse of the funds. However, with any such programme there is an inevitable trade-off between increasing administrative overheads and efficiency.

School Enrolment in India, Sri Lanka and Thailand 121

As a footnote to the discussion of primary enrolment in India some information is also available on the enrolment in primary education in Bangladesh by income group. Using four *per capita* income groups the observations were made in a recent village survey (see Table 7.5).

Table 7.5: Enrolment in Primary Education in Bangladesh

Enrolment from families with eligible children	Income group Rs			
	−200	201-300	301-400	400+
None	69	65	31	14
Some	10	6	6	4
All	21	29	63	82

Source: T. Islam, *Social Justice and the Education System of Bangladesh* (Dacca, 1973).

It is interesting to note in these data that while the share of families with all eligible children (aged 6-10) enrolled in school rises with income group, the share of those families with some children enrolled falls. Generally, the author of the book from which the information is taken[25] points out there is a polarisation with either all or no children enrolled: in only a few families are some eligible children in school and some not. In this study the author attributes the low enrolment rate of children from poorer families to poverty, i.e. to the need to cover out-of-pocket expenses and the possibility of making profitable use of children's labour. One point made by the author in relation to Bangladesh is that high apparent drop-out rates in the early grades may well be the direct result of exaggerated and fictitious reports of high enrolment in Grade I. To what extent this observation may apply elsewhere, and is indeed correct for Bangladesh, is unknown. It is likely, however, that attendance in the lower grades may be highly irregular and certain enrolment figures therefore illusory.

School Enrolment and Attendance in Sri Lanka

Together with the Philippines, Sri Lanka is frequently held up as an example of educational progress and educational egalitarianism. In relation to many Asian countries this is correct, especially as regards the schooling of teenagers. However, there are many problems of school attendance and retention in school in Sri Lanka that affect future income distribution and which, one can be sure, are magnified in countries with less egalitarian educational structures.

Table 7.6 first of all shows school enrolment for children in even-year age groups ranked into quintiles of *per capita* household income. For each income group except the very poorest, enrolment rates peak at the age of 8 years. The very poorest have a tendency to enter school late. For all age groups enrolment rates nearly always rise with income level. One can study a variety of transition rates, or rather the ratios of enrolment between different age groups. It would appear that broadly the effect of income is strongest in the transition between the ages 10 and 16; in the richest group two-thirds of the ten-year-old enrolment is still at school at the age of 16; for the poorest group only some 40 per cent remains. For other transition rates, e.g. 8-14 or 14-18, variations between income groups are not so marked. The enrolment rates can be inverted to show that at least 5 per cent of the children of the rich never attend school, and that at the age of 14 some 30 per cent of them are out of school. For the poorest group some 15 per cent never attend school; but at the age of 18 nearly 25 per cent of the children of the poorest group are still at school. This is no mean national achievement.

Table 7.6: School Enrolment by Age and *Per Capita* Household Income* (per cent)

Income quintile	Age of pupils						
	6	8	10	12	14	16	18
0- 20	69.9	83.6	85.0	70.9	59.2	36.0	23.7
20- 40	75.2	91.6	88.7	79.3	66.4	46.3	23.2
40- 60	81.1	92.3	88.0	82.1	68.6	48.3	24.8
60- 80	74.5	91.7	90.9	85.8	77.2	55.2	30.2
80-100	87.2	94.7	89.2	83.4	70.4	59.5	35.2

*Data from this source relate to regular school attendance in the month preceding the (four round) survey.
Source: Department of Census and Statistics, *Socio-Economic Survey of Sri Lanka, 1969-70*.

Table 7.7 has been constructed to allow comparison with Table 7.2 showing enrolment and retention rates in West Bengal by quintile group. It therefore also shows broad male and female rates separately and urban and rural rates separately. Given the circumstances of Sri Lanka, enrolment rates have been given for rural areas including estate areas, and for estate areas separately. The latter figures are no doubt

School Enrolment in India, Sri Lanka and Thailand 123

vitiated by a tendency of higher income groups to acquire secondary schooling for their children in non-estate areas.

Except in relation to the richest groups in urban areas (for both boys and girls) the Sri Lanka rates are far above the West Bengal rates. The gap between the richest and the poorest is of a totally different order of magnitude. In West Bengal there is a tremendous gap between rural and urban for females at the younger level, whatever the income group. This is missing in Sri Lanka. In West Bengal rural areas there is a large gap between males and females except at the richest level. This is also missing in Sri Lanka. Some of the retention rates in West Bengal are, however, higher than in Sri Lanka.

Given all this, there are certain tendencies apparent in both Sri Lanka and West Bengal. Female enrolment rates are generally below male rates and female retention rates are below male retention rates. Enrolment rates rise with income group, most markedly, as in West Bengal, for rural girls in the older age group. The Sri Lanka rates for estates only are uniformly below the rates for rural areas including estates. The greatest difference is for females in the 15-17 age group, only a handful of whom are still at school in estate areas. In the 6-14 age group estate enrolment ratios for boys and girls are nevertheless significantly higher than in rural West Bengal.

How, it can also be asked, has school attendance by income group changed in Sri Lanka in recent years? A survey made in 1959[26] can be contrasted with the results of the 1969-70 socio-economic survey, as in Table 7.8. The data are for six household income groups, of which, for the sake of brevity, only the poorest, middle and richest are represented in the table. The income ranges cover the same percentages of households for both dates.

The general impression created by Table 7.8 is that there was little change between 1959 and 1969, the pattern being the same in both years. Enrolment rates were in fact lower in 1969 for the ages of 6 and 8 years and higher for the age of 14. Children would appear to be both starting and leaving school at a slightly higher age than before. Given that income appears particularly influential in affecting retention rates for younger teenagers, this may be a welcome trend. In fact, contrasting the retention rates from the ages of 8 to 14 in both years, the increase was greatest for the lowest income group. But overall the decade 1959-69 saw the same income-enrolment patterns, which suggests that the problems which persist are particularly recalcitrant.

The 1959 survey also covered reasons for non-attendance. The general report on the survey contains few conclusions except that

Table 7.7: Enrolment and Retention Rates: Rural, Estate and Urban Areas, 1969 (per cent)

Quintile group	Rural* Males			Rural* Females			Estate Males			Estate Females			Urban Males			Urban Females		
	I	II	II/I	I	II	II/I	I	II	II/I	I	II	II/I	I	II	II/I	I	II	II/I
0- 20	80	43	54	71	32	45	59	21	36	47	9	19	83	56	67	85	42	50
20- 40	84	44	53	79	38	47	73	26	36	57	7	12	88	57	65	83	45	54
40- 60	87	55	63	81	44	54	76	33	43	63	14	22	92	59	65	88	49	55
60- 80	85	55	65	82	50	61	73	25	—	59	11	18	93	71	76	87	50	57
80-100	90	61	68	85	59	70	76	8	—	63	22	35	87	71	82	87	62	72

*Including estate.
I = age group 6-14; II = age group 15-17; II/I = the ratio of the enrolment rates of the two age groups.
Source: Department of Census and Statistics, *Socio-Economic Survey*.

Table 7.8: Enrolment by Age and Household Income, 1959-69 (per cent)

Household income	Age of pupils				
	6	8	10	12	14
1959					
Poorest[1]	77.3	82.6	75.8	67.6	34.5
Middle[2]	82.5	91.0	86.1	71.7	57.4
Richest[3]	95.9	98.3	98.3	91.2	86.3
Average	*83.0*	*91.0*	*85.8*	*71.7*	*55.3*
1969					
Poorest[1]	62.1	77.3	80.2	58.7	44.1
Middle[2]	74.6	89.0	85.5	80.4	64.2
Richest[3]	93.1	96.2	90.1	86.0	73.0
Average	*75.9*	*89.4*	*87.0*	*79.4*	*66.7*

[1] 0-9.3 per cent (In 1959 these were income groups Rs 0-25, Rs 51-75
[2] 39.4-64.2 per cent and Rs 200+; for 1969 the equivalent percentages were
[3] 93.4-100 per cent used.)
Sources: *Report of the Committee on Non-School-Going Children*, SP III (Colombo, 1960), and Department of Census and Statistics, *Socio-Economic Survey*.

'contrary to popular belief, lack of schools is not one of the major problems of non-attendance'. In the recommendations of the report stress is laid on greater compulsion in school attendance and the need for more imaginative curricula. In a questionnaire given to parents of 5,140 children of school age not attending school there was a choice of 34 responses. Taking only the primary response these can be categorised as follows:

(a) Poverty: 40 per cent. (Includes 'parents cannot afford to maintain children in school', 'cannot afford to buy books' etc.)
(b) Relative priorities: 31 per cent. (These factors may be the corollary of poverty, but not necessarily, i.e. 'parents find continued education not worth while', 'wish the children to help them at home', 'home circumstances are so difficult'.)
(c) Unsuitable curriculum: 9 per cent. (This includes 'pupils do not consider education worth while'.)
(d) Illness and physical handicaps: 7 per cent.
(e) Physical access: 4 per cent. (Includes no schools within two miles, no transport, no roads in remote areas.)
(f) Other: 9 per cent.

As one might expect, poverty emerges as the most important single factor, but given the extent of non-attendance among the rich, it probably does not, in this context, account for even a majority of the cases of non-attendance.

Table 7.9: Age and Level of Education Attained (per cent)

Age and level of education	Section A[1] Income group			Section B[2] Income group		
	1[3]	2[4]	3[5]	1	2[4]	3[5]
12 Primary	65	51	37	57	44	29
Middle	35	49	63	43	56	71
13 Primary	53	33	28	43	26	16
Middle	47	67	72	57	74	84
14 Primary	42	36	23	26	22	4
Middle	57	64	75	73	78	93
'O' level	1	–	2	1	–	3
15 Primary	41	29	18	14	12	4
Middle	59	69	79	86	86	93
'O' level	1	1	3	–	1	3
16 Primary	41	31	21	16	6	3
Middle	57	66	71	81	87	86
'O' level	2	4	8	2	6	10
17 Primary	36	30	19	11	5	2
Middle	58	65	62	76	86	70
'O' level	4	4	18	11	9	27
'A' level	2	–	1	2	–	1
18 Primary	41	32	30	8	–	1
Middle	54	57	48	82	74	57
'O' level	5	11	21	10	26	39
'A' level	–	–	1	–	–	3

Key: [1] All children who ever attended school.
[2] Children in school.
[3] Poorest quintile.
[4] Middle quintile.
[5] Richest quintile.
Source: Department of Census and Statistics, *Socio-Economic Survey*.

Table 7.9, which gives data only for the poorest, middle and richest *per capita* income groups, shows, for all children who ever attended school, how their educational mix changes with age. Section A covers children in and out of school and Section B children in school only. Section A shows how at ages 12 and 13 the children of the rich are far more likely to be in the middle than the primary grades; at age 14 the poor have more nearly caught up. From age 15 onwards to age 18 the educational structure of the group of poorer children changes very little. For the richer children, however, the shift from the middle grades

School Enrolment in India, Sri Lanka and Thailand

to secondary grades accelerates.

Section B of Table 7.9 relates, as noted, only to children in school. One immediate point is that the 'high-flyers', those reaching 'O' level at the age of 14, or 'A' level at the age of 17, form a very similar proportion of all income groups. In the early years (12, 13, 14), it takes the poorest group a couple of years to catch up with the educational pattern of the richest group. In some respects the poorest group never catches up. At the age of 14 only 4 per cent of the richest group are still in primary school. At the age of 18 the poorest group still has nearly 8 per cent of its members in primary grades and unlike the richest group, the poorest never reaches the proportion of over 40 per cent in secondary school. The data lead to the suspicion that not only do the poor start school later and leave earlier but they may also make their way more slowly up the educational ladder (the large share in middle grades represents to some extent the difficulty of passing the 'O' level hurdle).

Table 7.10 is interesting in this and other respects. It shows, again by three income groups, the poorest, middle and richest quintiles, the share of children with a particular education level who are in school. For primary grades the table shows the interesting results that children of the rich who have done no better than reach primary level by the age of 14 are very unlikely to be still at school. Curiously it is the middle-income group which shows the greatest persistence in the face of this relative education failure.

Table 7.10: Children in School by Grade Attained and Income (per cent)

Age	Primary Income group			Middle Income group			'O' level Income group		
	1^1	2^2	3^3	1^1	2^2	3^3	1^1	2^2	3^3
12	69	75	67	96	97	99	–	n.a.	–
13	61	68	47	90	94	96	–	n.a.	–
14	42	44	13	87	89	92	100	–	100
15	18	28	15	74	83	88	–	85	100
16	17	10	9	61	69	76	–	96	85
17	11	7	7	47	56	65	96	89	85
18	5		1	40	35	43	48	63	79

[1] Poorest quintile.
[2] Middle quintile.
[3] Richest quintile.
Source: Department of Census and Statistics, *Socio-Economic Survey*.

128 *School Enrolment in India, Sri Lanka and Thailand*

For middle grades the results are much as expected: persistence rises with income level, and the share still at school falls with age. The results for 'O' level are more mixed, but the picture for the age of 18 at any rate is discouraging: even the educationally fairly successful children of the poor are less likely to be continuing in school (to achieve 'A' levels and perhaps university entrance) than the children of the rich.

The Sri Lanka Ministry of Education's *Medium Term Plan for the Development of Education, 1973-1977* gives certain data on education by district which can be used to throw light on the role of certain educational supply variables in retaining children in school. The data show, by district, the ratios of the numbers in Grade VI over Grade II[27] and in Grade X over Grade VI. The first ratios are broadly the rates of retention in middle and lower secondary education. The first ratio varies from over 70 per cent in Colombo to 40 and below in Mannar, Vavuniya, Trincomalee and Kulmunai educational districts. The second ratio varies much less although it reaches over 100 in Galle, Jaffna and Kegalle and drops to around 50 per cent in Mannar. The values of the second ratio are in every case higher than those of the first.

Other data by district are available for (a) repetition in Grade 1; (b) pupils per school; (c) the proportion of schools with classes spanning only Grades I to V; (d) the proportion of graduate teachers in the total; (e) the proportion of 'other' teachers, i.e. neither graduate nor trained, in the total; and (f) population density. Repetition in Grade I can be very high: it is over 40 per cent in Anuradhapura, Trincomalee, Batticaloa and Kalmunai but as low as 17 per cent in South Colombo. The Ministry of Education[28] considers that these extreme variations must be caused by local conditions, although they are not sure which. The number of pupils per school, usually around 250-350, reaches nearly 800 in South Colombo and falls to under 200 in Anuradhapura, Vavuniya, Mannar and Batticaloa.

It is possible to work out some rank correlations of the two ratios, Grade VI over Grade II and Grade X over Grade VI, with these other variables. These are as follows:

Ratio Grade VI over Grade II, retention in primary education, with selected variables:

(a) Absence of repetition in Grade I: 0.745.
(b) Pupils per school: 0.764.
(c) Proportion of schools spanning more than Grades I-V: 0.701.
(d) Proportion of 'other' teachers: −0.133.
(e) Population density: 0.810.

School Enrolment in India, Sri Lanka and Thailand

Ratio Grade X over Grade VI, repetition in middle and lower secondary education, with selected variables:

(a) Absence of repetition in Grade I: 0.528.
(b) Pupils per school: 0.575.
(c) Proportion of graduate teachers: 0.389.
(d) Population density: 0.680.

Generally, the coefficients are higher for the first set of variables. In this interdistrict comparison the composition of the teaching force does not appear so very important. In each case school size, which will vary considerably with population density,[29] is important, as is repetition or its absence in Grade I. It is likely that districts with greater Grade I repetition are those with more irregular school attendance and are generally in the least urbanised and east coast areas. There is also a correlation between size of school and absence of repetition in Grade I of $R = 0.7$, i.e. there is more likely to be repetition in smaller schools.

If a composite index of the ratio of Grade VI over Grade II and of repetition in Grade I were constructed to demonstrate the power of primary schools in retaining their pupils, there would be four obvious 'underprivileged' districts: Anuradhapura, Kalmunai, Trincomalee and Batticaloa; and six relatively 'privileged' districts: South and North Colombo, Kalutara, Galle, Matara and Kegalle. There is no doubt that, in general, it is the relative isolation of the population of the former districts which is important. This seems to result in a large number of relatively small schools and considerable early repetition. This no doubt will in any event discourage persistence in education.

One more point to be mentioned is the extent to which parental education levels and occupations affect children's school enrolment independently of household income levels. There is no doubt that such effects do exist, as the data collected in 1959 for enrolment by parental education group can show. Those data have the advantage over the similar 1969 results of giving a finer breakdown of parents' education levels. Results can be tabulated both for fathers' and mothers' education levels; they are very similar and only the latter are given here (Table 7.11). The effects can be seen to be quite substantial, particularly at lower and middle income levels.

The results of the 1969-70 socio-economic survey can be manipulated to yield results on enrolment by occupational group of head of household[30] and by income group. The income groups used are the quintiles as before, established on an all-island basis. The data are given

Table 7.11: Per Cent Enrolled by Mothers' Education Level and Household Income

Income group	Mothers' education level (grades)					
	Nil	I+II	III+IV	V+VI	VII+VIII	IX+
Poorest	63.7	65.3	77.5	82.4	89.0	77.8
Middle	73.7	77.0	83.3	87.6	89.3	96.0
Richest	90.8	86.4	94.9	93.5	98.5	97.1

Source: *Report of the Committee on Non-School-Going Children.*

separately in Tables 7.12 and 7.13: Table 7.12 covers the ages of 7 to 10 years inclusive and Table 7.13 the ages of 14 to 17 inclusive.

Reading from left to right, one finds the data in Table 7.12 sometimes surprising, partly because of the small size of some of the cells. It must be recalled that in Table 7.6 the highest enrolment rate recorded was 95 per cent; no doubt 100 per cent must be considered a freak result. However, one can conclude that the influence of income, or lack of income, is greatest for the occupation groups of cultivators, other agriculture and sales. Reading downwards the effect of occupation within the two highest income groups would seem negligible. Among the lower income groups this is not so; for professional and clerical groups and also for many worker groups rates are also high. However, the differences between occupations will also reflect education levels of parents and probably the urban-rural split also.

Table 7.12 also includes a column giving the average of the income group figures, thus eliminating most of the effects of income. The results are broadly as expected, with a particularly high rating for transport workers.

Table 7.13 differs in certain respects from Table 7.12. Above all, the average figures show a far greater spread than before. Reading from left to right, i.e. viewing the effects of income on occupation group, it appears that poverty is far more important as a factor restricting enrolment of teenagers than it was for younger children, for clerical workers, cultivators, production workers and service workers. The poor groups in these occupations have noticeably lower enrolment rates than the richer groups. Poverty among other groups such as professionals, other agriculture workers and transport workers would not seem to reduce enrolment rates below the customary level for those occupations. Reading downwards it appears that even among the richer groups, other agriculture workers, production workers and workers in services have

School Enrolment in India, Sri Lanka and Thailand

Table 7.12: Enrolment of Children Aged 7-10 by Occupation of Head of Household (per cent)

Occupation group	Quintile income group					Average**
	I*	II	III	IV	V	
Professional and related	100	100	87	100	96	*97*
Teachers	n.a.	n.a.	n.a.	100	93	*97*
Clerical	100	99	96	90	89	*97*
Sales	81	93	92	90	93	*90*
Cultivators	85	88	87	92	93	*89*
Other agriculture	74	81	81	90	94	*84*
Transport	94	97	97	97	99	*97*
Production	91	96	94	92	93	*93*
Services	92	96	89	84	97	*92*

*Poorest 20 per cent etc.
**Unweighted.
Source: Department of Census and Statistics, *Socio-Economic Survey*.

Table 7.13: Enrolment of Children Aged 14-17 by Occupation of Head of Household (per cent)

Occupation group	Quintile income group					Average*
	I	II	III	IV	V	
Professional and related	71	n.a.	81	90	63	*76*
Teachers	n.a.	n.a.	n.a.	72	73	*73*
Clerical	56	72	78	84	74	*73*
Sales	62	59	64	70	68	*65*
Cultivators	48	51	54	70	60	*57*
Other agriculture	36	38	35	29	27	*33*
Transport	85	67	77	73	63	*73*
Production	42	48	60	53	62	*53*
Services	38	53	60	56	56	*53*

*Unweighted.
Source: Department of Census and Statistics, *Socio-Economic Survey*.

noticeably low enrolment rates in this age bracket.

University Admission in Sri Lanka

So far we have studied enrolment and in-school promotion in Sri Lanka up to the terminal secondary level. In addition we can examine data on university enrolment in terms of certain population groups at two points of time and other information on students' household background and course of university study.

Sri Lanka is a multi-ethnic country: the predominant population group consists of Sinhalese, who are nearly all either Buddhist or Christian, followed by Ceylon and Indian Tamils, either Hindu or Christian, with smaller groups of Moslems and Burghers (generally Christian). The Christian denomination tends to be closely associated with urban areas and with low-country wet zone areas and more loosely associated with higher than average income groups. Among the richer groups the Christian denomination was associated with knowledge, and use, of the English language. Table 7.14 shows the breakdown of the total population by these groups in the early 1950s and late 1960s, and university admission in 1950 and 1967.

Table 7.14: Population and University Admission, Sri Lanka (per cent)

Population group	Proportion of population		Proportion of admissions	
	1950	1967	1950	1967
Sinhalese Buddhists	64.3	66.3	48.6	79.2
Sinhalese Christians	5.2	4.7	18.0	4.9
Ceylon Tamil Hindus	7.5	7.8	15.6	10.8
Ceylon Tamil Christians	3.4	3.3	8.9	3.3
Indian Tamils*	12.4	10.6	1.4	0.1
Moslems	6.0	6.7	1.9	1.4
Burghers and others	1.2	0.6	5.6	0.3
Total	100.0	100.0	100.0	100.0

*It is assumed that no Indian Tamils are Christian.
Source: Uswatte Arachchi, *Modern Asian Studies*, July 1974.

In the early 1950s when most secondary and all university education was in English the various Christian groups, as well as Ceylon Tamil Hindus, were proportionately overrepresented in university admission. Sinhalese Buddhists were significantly underrepresented, as were Indian Tamils and to a lesser extent Moslems. These last two groups continued to be considerably underrepresented into the late 1960s: education facilities for Indian Tamils failed to improve, and many Moslems had an ambivalent attitude towards university education.

Almost certainly the main change during the period 1950-67 was the extension of instruction in Sinhalese to nearly all secondary schools and to the university. Language streaming still permitted instruction in Tamil and in English for Burghers, a few others, and those Moslems who chose it. By 1967 university admissions for Christian groups reflected very closely their population shares. Sinhalese Buddhists obviously made great strides and by 1967 were overrepresented.

However, whereas Sinhalese-language secondary education expanded quickly, there remained considerable differences in the efficiency of various schools in passing their pupils into the most desired university courses of study. In 1967 admission to various university faculties had a household income bias, as Table 7.15 shows.

Table 7.15: Income Group Origins and Admission to Various Faculties in Sri Lanka

Faculty	Up to Rs 300 a month	Greater than Rs 300 a month
Humanities and social studies	31.02	5.45
Law	13.06	16.36
Science	15.10	18.18
Medicine and dentistry	6.53	24.74
Agriculture and veterinary medicine	20.00	16.00
Engineering	14.29	19.27
Total	100.00	100.00

Source: Figures calculated from Arachchi, *Modern Asian Studies*, p. 308.

Children from poorer households were nearly six times more likely to be studying humanities and social studies and nearly four times less likely to be studying medicine and dentistry. There is no doubt at all that in Sri Lanka and most other developing countries members of the medical profession have higher earnings and far better prospects than graduates in the humanities and in social studies. The latter, unless they receive a first class or upper second class degree, have unexciting prospects (mainly as school teachers). Thus admission to the medical faculty, and to a lesser extent to the engineering faculty, is sufficient to ensure a privileged place in the upper reaches of the income distribution and considerable social status. In commenting on the origins of various students, Uswatte Arachchi states,

> most students entering the humanities and social studies faculties came from Maha and Madhya Maha Vidyalayas. In contrast, among other faculties, their proportion was quite small: 5 per cent in law, 15 per cent in science, 4 per cent in medicine and dentistry, 15 per cent in agriculture and veterinary science and 12 per cent in engineering. The admissions to these faculties were dominated by students

from 'other government' and private schools . . .[31]

Sex Disparities in Admissions

In the IEA studies, sex differences in scholastic achievement were shown to have a cultural basis. Social expectations and career opportunities were implied to have an influence on interest as well as on achievement in certain subjects. Exposure to learning opportunities in science, for example, was used to explain sex differences in achievement in that subject, which were observed to widen with time spent in school. This was true both in developing and advanced countries, and it seems to hold good in Sri Lanka.

We have seen that female enrolment rates for secondary education in Sri Lanka are below the rates for males, although not by much. Overall access to the university reflects this. However, the sex mix varies greatly between faculties (see Table 7.16). Humanities and social studies is the only course with female over-representation. Law and medicine have shares of female students not far below this overall proportion. Science, engineering and agriculture are all faculties where women are underrepresented. This mix must reflect a certain cultural bias, which may, however, have shown up already during secondary schooling, by e.g. school science facilities being used more by boys than girls.

Table 7.16: Sex Disparities in University Admissions, Sri Lanka, 1967 (per cent)

Faculty	Females	Males
All	47	53
Humanities and social studies	52	48
Law	45	55
Science	31	69
Medicine and dentistry	43	57
Agriculture and veterinary medicine	19	81
Engineering	3	97

Source: Arachchi, *Modern Asian Studies*, p. 292.

Geographical Disparities

Not only were there ethnic, religious and sex disparities, there were also regional inequalities in access to higher education in Sri Lanka. Records of university admission in 1967 showed that, on regional parity based on population (1963), one-quarter of all districts had more than their share of university places. Among more than 20 districts, five (Kalutara, Galle, Jaffna, Colombo and Matara) had more than they should have, while the rest had much less. One in fact had no one admitted to the university during that year (Mannar).

These regional imbalances in university admission can have tremendous impact on future employment (and income) opportunities of those who were admitted (and finally completed schooling) as well as on those who failed to get admission and on those who dropped out of the educational rat race. These imbalances generally reflect the differences that were noted earlier in terms of retention and repetition in primary schooling. Of the districts mentioned there as 'privileged', only one, Kegalle, is not over-represented at the university. However, to the 'underprivileged' districts mentioned there others should be added, e.g. Puttalam and Moneragala. The pattern, however, is the same. Thus, attempts in Sri Lanka to institute a district quota system in university admission are merely a reaction to disparities which began long before. The district quota system which was introduced (and has now been withdrawn) was severely criticised, even if the concept may have some merits.[32]

Thailand

The information that is presented in this section mainly concerns secondary schools in a system which requires seven years of primary schooling and a national examination. Secondary schools in Thailand form two tiers, lower secondary and upper secondary. In the first education is common, whereas the second consists of specialised streams, e.g. academic and vocational. Admission to any of these streams is obtained by passing a national examination which determines who goes to which type of upper secondary school. Generally, the better scorers in that examination enter the academic stream in preparation for university studies.[33]

Regional Disparities in Secondary School Attendance

Taking the population figures of 1970 as proxies for 1975 and utilising them as basis for parity distribution of secondary school enrolment, it can be shown that the Bangkok metropolitan area had school attendance which is much higher than the parity line, especially at the upper secondary level (see Table 7.17).

Among provinces there are also wide deviations from parity. These

136 *School Enrolment in India, Sri Lanka and Thailand*

Table 7.17: Regional Disparities in Secondary School Enrolment, Thailand (per cent)

	Population 1970	Enrolment 1975	*Difference*
Total			
Bangkok area	8.9	21.1	*+136.2*
Provinces	91.1	78.9	*– 13.4*
Lower secondary			
Bangkok area	8.9	17.9	*+100.3*
Provinces	91.1	82.1	*– 9.9*
Upper secondary			
Bangkok area	8.9	41.8	*+366.8*
Provinces	91.1	58.2	*– 36.1*

Source: Calculated from data supplied by World Bank Report, Thailand, 1976, citing Ministry of Education, 1976.

are shown simply and sharply by aggregating the provinces into regions. The figures in Table 7.18 indicate that on the whole, the Central region (including Bangkok metropolitan area) and the South regions had better school attendance or enrolment rates than the North and Northeast regions. This observation is especially true at the lower secondary level and to a limited extent at the upper level. The North, and particularly the North-east, have rates which are much lower than those of the rest of Thailand.

Table 7.18: Regional Disparities in Secondary School Enrolment, Thailand (per cent)

Region	Percentage difference from population parity		
	Lower	Upper*	All
Central	+21.5	–11.6	+17.0
South	+5.4	–8.4	+3.5
North	–20.4	–39.2	–25.2
North-east	–27.4	–59.6	–31.7

*All rates below parity due to predominance of Bangkok area.
Source: Figures calculated from World Bank Report, Thailand, 1976, citing Ministry of Education and National Economic Council as source, Annex 4.

Figures on enrolment rates, i.e. the proportion of relevant age groups attending school, show disparities which are more stark, especially if we use the data on the Bangkok metropolitan area as the reference point. For example, 42 per cent of 14 to 16 year olds in Bangkok are attending lower secondary school, whereas in the provinces the proportion is only 21 per cent. The corresponding rates for the upper secondary school are 23 per cent and 4 per cent for Bangkok and provinces respectively. Among the regions we find the same situation as that described earlier: the North-east has the lowest rates of all the regions, followed by the North and South, whereas the rates for the Central region around Bangkok are generally high (see Table 7.19).

Table 7.19: Enrolment Ratios in Thailand Secondary Schools, 1975 (per cent)

	Lower	Upper
Grand total	23.0	6.0
Bangkok metropolitan area	42.0	23.0
Provincial total	21.0	4.0
Regions:* Central	27.7	4.7
South	24.0	6.3
North	18.0	3.5
North-east	17.7	2.7

*Unweighted averages of provincial data.
Source: Calculated from World Bank Report, Thailand, 1976, Annex 4, pp. 1f.

The enrolment data show only the tip of an iceberg. Expenditure per pupil in the lower primary schools in 1970 indicates that pupils in Bangkok received much more educational resources — in fact many times more (e.g. better teachers and facilities) than those in the North-east or the North. This widely disparate distribution (see Table 7.20) changed somewhat in 1972 toward an amelioration of the differences, but Bangkok pupils still received more than twice as much as pupils in the North-east. In terms of specific educational resources such as textbooks, the pattern is the same. Of the primary school pupils in Bangkok, 92 per cent had the required books in Thai and arithmetic, whereas the figure for the North-east is a mere 65 per cent. All these differences (or inequalities) in educational resource distribution have their effects on scholastic achievement.

Average test scores of primary school pupils in Thai language decline sharply from Bangkok toward its perimeter region, i.e. the Central region, then onwards to the South and North, and finally to the North-east which has the lowest average scores. The pattern of average test scores in arithmetic is practically the same as that in Thai. These patterns are obviously due not to chance variables but most probably to the systematic effects of causal factors such as the variation or the

138 *School Enrolment in India, Sri Lanka and Thailand*

shape of the distribution of educational resources, as well as to nonschool factors that were reported by the IEA studies.

Indeed, Bangkok is distinctly different from the rest of the country in terms of schooling. Using regions as units of analysis, we find that school enrolment rates vary widely. Bangkok comes consistently first, the Central and South regions come next, while the rest of Thailand is virtually deprived. Provision of educational resources follows the same pattern. All this had an inevitable consequence in the distribution of scholastic achievement. What Thorndike found between developing and advanced countries seems to exist also between Bangkok and provinces of Thailand, i.e. that by the standards of Bangkok, the schoolchildren in the provinces seem illiterate.

Low attendance rates and low scholastic achievement in the provinces in contrast with those in Bangkok suggest that educational deprivation in the former, and above all in the North-east, is notably more severe than is usually imagined.

Table 7.20: Educational Disparity in Thailand

Criterion	Bangkok metropolitan area	Central region (including Bangkok)	South region	North region	North-east region
Capital expenditure per pupil in Baht, lower primary schools					
1970	160	107	107	69	47
1972	119	119	104	79	51
Percentage of pupils possessing required books in Thai and arithmetic	92	88	84	69	65
Average primary school achievement test scores:					
Thai language	51	34	31	29	26
Arithmetic	51	33	34	30	25

Source: World Bank Report, Thailand, 1976, citing data from the Ministry of Education and the National Economic Council.

Educational Policy-making

The data in this chapter and the last call for some comments on the process of policy-making in education. How did such inequality arise?

School Enrolment in India, Sri Lanka and Thailand 139

Why are some groups so obviously deprived? To represent education, or rather opportunities for school attendance, as something which all segments of society are falling over themselves in their hurry to obtain, is a distortion of the current picture in large parts of Asia. Frequently, as in certain parts of India or on the estates in Sri Lanka, education is not compulsory, not because attendance is already universal, but because it could not be enforced. Of course, there is no doubt that children can contribute to the household income; and also that poverty can keep children away from school and that their parents may deeply regret the lost opportunities. On the other hand, in many Asian countries the curriculum is unattractive, irregular attendance appears to be frequently condoned and the combination of conditions at school and at home makes it easy for children to drop out. In such circumstances the very poor are unlikely to be the most vociferous in demanding increased education facilities.

The distribution of educational expenditure is subject to a great deal of popular pressure, to which different sections of society contributed in varying degrees. But this pressure, which would frequently seem to have allowed the periphery to lead the centre, has by and large not produced great clashes with governments and their servants; while the periphery may have led the way, the governments have been apparently willing to provide schools, funds, grants-in-aid etc. There are strong reasons to suppose that the last 20-odd years have seen an alliance between politicians and civil servants on the one hand and certain increasingly dominant groups on the other. This has taken place against a background of a 'manpower requirements' approach to educational planning which gave considerable support to the expansion of secondary education. Obviously primary education has also expanded, but whatever intellectual leadership there may have been in favour of ensuring universal primary education before developing secondary education has presumably lacked sufficiently powerful allies. For example, the Ministry of Education in Sri Lanka would appear to worry more about the 100,000 pupils who leave school after Grade X (and who are to be given pre-vocational training in Grade IX to help them find respectable jobs) than about the 185,000 who annually leave school at an earlier stage.

There is little doubt that had more funds been devoted to primary education, drop-outs at earlier levels would have been less numerous. But what was needed was not, or only rarely, 'more of the same'. It is presumably the lesson to be learned from the persistence of low enrolment rates among the poor, even in metropolitan areas, that availability of educational facilities, even of neighbourhood education facilities, is not enough to attract children to school and to keep them there. Greater compulsion is, of course, one response, but not one that is usually attractive to a Ministry of Education. Yet had more money been spent on more attractive curricula, more books, more subsidies, scholarships at earlier levels and other incentives to overcome lack of interest on the part of parents and children, the results would no doubt have been worth while. Of course, lack of interest is very likely to be a sign of despair. Different income groups may see the possibilities of social mobility and the role of education in social mobility in a different light. Those at the top can size up for themselves the value of persisting with education. Those in the middle may put strong stress on achieving high education levels and then be disappointed in their search for appropriate jobs. Those at the bottom often know they cannot win.

Some obvious indices of the degree of non-government involvement in education include such factors as the importance of income from fees charged, the extent of privately financed education and the role of private management. All these indicators have to be seen within an education system in which publicly set and marked examinations at the national or provincial level give an acceptable set of credentials. The aspiration of parents, when expressed, is usually that their children should finish secondary school. Five or six years of education, i.e. completing the primary level, would not usually appear to be a desired goal. In an Indian slum[34] fully 80 per cent of parents questioned wanted their children to finish secondary school, if not to become university graduates. Yet, even in Sri Lanka, considerably more children leave school before entering the secondary cycle than after. Satisfaction at achieving primary education cannot be ruled out, nor correspondingly can pressure on the authorities to provide increased primary school facilities. It is, however, most likely that (a) although of a low standard, primary school facilities are generally available and (b) ministries can be relied on to provide such facilities without too much prompting.

The Indian Education Commission, for example, considered that 'the objective of universal provision of school facilities at the lower primary stage [Grades I-IV] has almost been reached. In almost all States, villages with a population of 300 or over are provided with school and, in several areas, even smaller villages have been given the facility.' Nevertheless, retention rates even to Grade IV are low, as low as 37 per cent in 1965-6. Of course, this could be called a misleading statistic, as many who leave after four years of schooling have never reached Grade IV. Thus, a 37 per cent retention rate is not an indicator of retention in any class. For example, data from Poona district, admittedly for as long ago as 1960, show that while 41 per cent of pupils left before completing Grade IV, the percentage not completing a fourth year was nearer 36 per cent. The Education Commission thus concluded that the major task ahead for primary education was 'to reduce stagnation and wastage to a minimum'. To the extent that what people were demanding was the supply of primary school facilities and the crudest physical possibility of building up years of primary education, the state would seem to have been meeting the demand.

The question then arises why people were apparently not demanding improvements in the quality of primary education. Presumably, given that 'quality' means a reduction of wastage and stagnation, this was not a matter that affected the relatively well-off. As our various sources of information have shown, the higher their parental income group, the greater the likelihood that children will work steadily through primary education. However, it can also be asked whether there is not a demand among those who have been forced to drop out of school, largely for reasons of poverty, for further part-time education, literacy courses etc. In the inquiry among tribal people it was noted that many who had dropped out were brought back into the system, full-time, by financial inducements. Otherwise, it is evident from the discussion of part-time classes in the Indian Education Commission's Report that despite strong support for the idea, very little was happening on the ground. It is impossible completely to avoid the conclusion, which is probably even more valid for Tamil schools on the estates in Sri Lanka,[35] that where prospects for occupational and social mobility are seen to be restricted, the demand and enthusiasm for education will be slight. Here we are referring to what are, in every sense, dependent communities, i.e. rural labourers in India or estate labourers in Sri Lanka.

Of course, it is very obvious that the desire to achieve and maintain literacy can vary not only between urban and rural areas, different income groups, different occupational groups etc. but between different rural areas, for example. The conceptions of a normal or standard level of education are affected by historical and traditional factors. Thus the very high literacy rates and retention rates in primary schooling in Kerala have been ascribed to 'the effect of a variety of earlier penetrations going back to the pre-Christian era. Not least among these influences is Christianity.'[36] Free mid-day meals in schools for 75 per cent of Kerala's 6-10-year-olds may also play a part.[37] The penetration of alien cultures can, of course, give an impetus to literacy and education. However, the impetus can again be towards taking up non-traditional avenues of social mobility — which were frequently opened by the advent of colonialism.[38]

The means by which public, or at least non-governmental, influence can be exerted on the organisation of the school system depend on the nature of the system. Of course, its peculiarities are often an outcome of disputes between the central authorities and local or other bodies at an earlier stage. Voluntary organisations which earlier had considerable control over school curricula, teachers' recruitment, examinations and other matters often gradually lose their power to central authorities. However, the extent of central direction varies from country to country. Sri Lanka, for example, has one of the most centralised of school systems, with least reliance on income from fees or local authority financial contributions and with decisions taken by a central ministry. In India and Bangladesh, on the other hand, the multiplicity of the system is due partly to differences between former princely states and British Territory and partly to pressures for local control through the Panchayat Raj system.

The Indian system is worth looking at in a little more detail since it demonstrates a certain form of decentralisation of control — although the major force of public examinations at the secondary level remains in government (state) hands. The Indian system permits privately managed schools which, primary and secondary taken together, were receiving some 37 per cent of their income from fees in the early 1960s. The corresponding figure for today is no doubt less. It also permits local-authority-managed schools, which received 26 per cent of their income from local funds. Primary schools are likely to be managed by the local authority; secondary schools to be privately managed. The Education Commission laid its finger on the weak spots of both these systems. Privately managed schools, when the teaching body is excluded from management, 'are dominated by sectarian considerations that affect the recruitment of teachers as well as their atmosphere. Several of them are run, not for purposes of education or social service, but for exploitation and patronage.' The local authority schools are involved with their communities but 'this generally proves to be not an asset but a disadvantage, because their teachers are often harassed through postings and transfers and become involved in local politics and factions'. The evil, apparently, increases as the delegation of authority extends to lower levels.

The decision to associate local authorities, especially in rural areas, with the administration of education was taken on political and not educational grounds, as a means of building up local democratic institutions. Frequently, however, it has become obvious that these authorities were far from democratic, and we have seen clearly the difference in the use made of primary facilities by the rural rich and the rural poor. However, it is easy to exaggerate the influence, for good or ill, of local politicians on education. Their influence is strongest in such matters as school location and teacher recruitment, and not in the content of schooling.[39]

The role, and indeed the consequences, of considerable private patronage in secondary education in Maharashtra State are discussed by Rosenthal.[40] He shows how private initiative, backed generally by grants-in-aid from the state, particularly where any political patronage was involved, extended secondary education into rural areas, although, as might naturally be expected, the quality of education was below that of urban schools. An announced Maharashtra State policy in 1970 to restrict the number of secondary schools offering an 'advanced' curriculum, which allowed college entrance, set off considerable opposition from village leaders. Tied to this was a suggestion to make the study of English compulsory from Grade VIII while the opposition, spearheaded by the Peasants and Workers' Party and the RSS (Peasant Education Society), which managed some 300 secondary schools, insisted it should be compulsory from Grade V. This whole debate, which finally the opposition won, was represented as an anti-elite dispute, directed against the traditional predominance of urban Brahmans in the civil service. However, it is quite clear, as Rosenthal points out, that disputes on whether to make English compulsory from Grade V or Grade VIII are disputes within an elite.

The role of private demand in the expansion of college education has been documented by Wood for Mysore.[41] Enrolments in private colleges under the university rose from 1,641 in 1947 to over 46,000 in 1967, while the earlier more important public colleges with an enrolment in 1947 of 8,575 had an enrolment of some 35,000 in 1967. As Wood states, 'while discrimination against Brahmans in government institutions was the single most important factor in the development of private colleges [i.e. by Brahmans] ... their success has encouraged other caste groups to enter the private sector'. However, he remarks that whereas caste groups were generally the most important initiators in this field, 'since Independence relationships between politicians and colleges have become even more common, and colleges have become one of the bases upon which a politician can build a career'. One result, however, was a mushrooming of small and ill-equipped colleges, since it was usually much easier to fund a college than to consolidate it.

It is the transparency of the role of private demand and private initiative in India, as revealed by these discussions, which is interesting. Private initiative can shape the educational system in other countries also, witness the discretion given to local authorities to set up barrio high schools in the Philippines. But in most other countries private initiative will work probably through the political system, or in Thailand through the provincial governor, and will then impinge directly on the funding or controlling ministry. That is to say that while other countries may operate what is certainly a highly centralised system, local demands for the expansion of secondary education will still be taken note of. And, as we have seen elsewhere, the same anti-traditional elite feeling may lead to restrictions on university entrance from some groups or areas. It must be said, however, that the authorities are much less responsive to private demand for the increase of college and university places in some countries than in others, however flexible they may be in respect of secondary education.

In this respect the Philippines would appear to present an example of the uncontrolled growth of secondary education with high schools, largely financed by tuition fees, set up at the barrio level whenever at least 40 pupils are forthcoming. The state allows the part-time use of services of elementary teachers. Nevertheless, one remarkable fact of Philippine occupational income statistics is that primary school teachers earn, on average, more than secondary teachers. A relatively cheap system of secondary education has presumably been obtained.

It is evident from the study carried out by G.T. Castillo and others[42] that dropping out of secondary school for extended periods is common. In a survey of three large villages or small towns, it was discovered that between a third and a half of in-school youth had dropped out at one stage or another, while among the out-of-school youth from 26 to 40 per cent aspired to a college degree, which meant returning to school. In one community 65 per cent of parents of out-of-school youth planned to send their children back to school. Of course, there is no doubt, as the study also shows, that expectations were sometimes not seriously held, and that parents often foresaw their children as becoming skilled workers at best even when they sought a college education for them. Furthermore, only some 20 to 40 per cent of the pupils who in fact completed secondary school would appear to reach college. There is therefore a certain amount of make-believe in approaches to secondary and college education. But again the survey clearly shows that it was in the most backward of the three areas studied that the

School Enrolment in India, Sri Lanka and Thailand 145

greatest reliance was placed on college education as a means of finding a good job and rising above village living standards. In more advanced areas alternative avenues for social mobility and wealth accumulation were seen. Thus, there is no doubt that a very considerable demand for high school education continues to be unfulfilled in poorer areas. But it was also clear that the quality of the education which these high schools were capable of giving was lowest in the poorer areas, where the certainty of their continued existence was also least.

Conclusions

Earlier it was suggested that obsession with concepts of manpower requirements had frequently paved the way for educational administrators to support the private demand for increased secondary enrolment. It would appear that from time to time education bodies have threatened to introduce stronger selection even to lower secondary education. Thus the Indian Education Commission stated: 'in order to restrict unplanned and uncontrolled expansion of secondary and higher education, it is necessary to restrict the provision for places in accordance with manpower estimates and to make the admissions on a selective basis'. However, this was little more than a paper threat, as can be seen in their projections for secondary school enrolment, which over the decade 1966-76 was expected to rise from 19 to 29 per cent for Grades VIII to X and from 7 to 11 per cent for Grades XI and XII; almost certainly increases of this nature have not occurred, and even with these projected enrolments the Commission still lamented that 'the proportion of educated and trained manpower would still be small, even in 1986'. It is not difficult to show by comparison with other countries that the capacity of any economy to absorb educated manpower should be much higher than it is.

It would naturally seem that the emergency of educated unemployment on a large scale would reduce the urge to educational expansion — both from the side of administrators and from consumers. Administrators indeed have sometimes reacted by stiffening selection procedures, for universities at least. At the secondary level the authorities are likely to respond by stressing the need to substitute vocational for academic curricula. Hence, for example, the stress in Sri Lanka on vocational education in junior secondary schools in the hope that more vocational education will make job-searching or job-creation easier.

On the consumer side it would sometimes appear that awareness of

146 *School Enrolment in India, Sri Lanka and Thailand*

the existence of unemployed college graduates acts as a brake to demand. A study in the Philippines found an inverse relation between parents' desire for a college education for their children and their awareness of graduate unemployment.[43] On the other hand, Rosenthal[44] quotes a representative of the expansionist RSS in Maharashtra as saying: 'No doubt we are producing many third class graduates, but that is still some advance on the former situation. They do swell the ranks of the unemployed but that is probably better than remaining unemployed and in a village wasting their time distilling illicit liquor.'

For Maharashtra, Rosenthal concluded that the approaches of the 'bureaucrat and politician appear to be complementary rather than in conflict'. He remarks that neither group speaks 'for the kind of egalitarianism which might involve a radical levelling of social groups'. This conclusion is probably applicable to a great deal of Asian educational policy, given the usual strong correlation between low incomes and dropping out of school.

Notes

1. D.G. Mandelbaum, *Society in India* (University of California Press, 1970).
2. National Council of Educational Research and Training, *Developmental Needs of the Tribal People* (New Delhi, 1971).
3. A.P. Barnabas, *Social Change in a North Indian Village* (Indian Institute of Public Administration, 1969).
4. A.R. Desai, *Profile of an Indian Slum* (Bombay, 1972).
5. T. Scarlett Epstein, *South India, Yesterday, Today and Tomorrow* (London, Macmillan, 1973).
6. Barnabas, *Social Change*.
7. Desai, *Indian Slum*.
8. D. Adams, *Education and Modernisation in Asia* (Wesley Publishing Co., 1970).
9. E.D. Driver, in *Social Forces*, Vol. XLI (1962).
10. Agricultural Economics Research Centre, University of Delhi, *Primary Education in Rural India* (Delhi, 1967). It was necessary to make slight adjustments to the published data to ensure comparability.
11. There could be other reasons for this apparent 'caste effect' such as a different age-sex composition for children of the two groups. This is unlikely, however.
12. T. Maitra *et al.*, *An Enquiry into the Distribution of Public Education and Health Services in West Bengal*.
13. National Council of Educational Research and Training, *Wastage and Stagnation in Primary and Middle Schools* (Delhi, 1968).
14. Ibid., p. 66.
15. Mandelbaum, *Society in India*.
16. *Education and National Development*, Report of the Education Com-

mission, 1964-6 (Delhi, 1966).

17. Suma Chitnis, *Literacy and Educational Enrolment Among the Scheduled Castes of Maharashtra* (Bombay, 1974).

18. Ibid.

19. *Report of the Commissioner for Scheduled Castes and for Scheduled Tribes, 1971-72 and 1972-73* (Delhi, 1974).

20. Suma Chitnis, *Maharashtra*.

21. *Report of the Commissioner*.

22. National Council of Educational Research and Training, *Utilization of Financial Assistance by Tribal Students* (Delhi, 1971).

23. Ibid.

24. Ibid., p. 150.

25. T. Islam, *Social Justice and the Education System of Bangladesh* (Dacca, 1973).

26. *Report of the Committee on Non-School-Going Children*, SP III (Colombo, 1960).

27. The previous year the age of school entry was raised; thus comparisons with Grade I were not possible.

28. Sri Lanka, Ministry of Education, *Medium Term Plan for the Development of Education, 1973-1977.*

29. Correlation pupils per school to population density: 0.870.

30. In fact the heads of household could not be identified. The data refer to the occupation of the first household member listed; that person was in the overwhelming majority of cases male and between 20 and 60 years of age.

31. Uswatte Arachchi, *Modern Asian Studies*, (July 1974).

32. See C.R. de Silva, 'Weightage in University Admissions: Standardisation and District Quotas in Sri Lanka 1970-1975', *Modern Ceylon Studies,* (July 1974).

33. In recent years, Thailand has been moving towards a comprehensive secondary school system and converting specialised vocational schools into technical schools or colleges.

34. Desai, *Indian Slum*.

35. See G.A. Gnanamuttu, *Education and the Indian Plantation Worker in Sri Lanka* (Colombo, 1977).

36. L.I. and S.H. Rudolph, *Economic and Political Weekly*, (1969).

37. *Poverty, Unemployment and Development Policy, A Case Study of Selected Issues with Reference to Kerala* (New York, United Nations, 1975). This study does not mention the matriarchal nature of much of Kerala society as a reason for the popularity of formal education; one wonders whether it played any role.

38. For an account of how certain coastal groups in Sri Lanka leap-frogged the traditional up-country elite at the start of the British period, see Michael Roberts, *Facets of Modern Ceylon History Through the Letters of Jeronis Pieris* (Colombo, 1975).

39. See D.B. Rosenthal, 'Policy Making: Maharashtra', *Comparative Education Review* (February 1974).

40. See ibid.

41. G. Wood, 'Planning University Reform, an Indian Case Study', *Comparative Education Review*, (June 1972).

42. G.T. Castillo et al., *Alternatives for Rural Youth* (University of the Philippines at Los Banos, Laguna, 1975).

43. Ibid.

44. Rosenthal, 'Policy Making: Maharashtra'.

8 EDUCATIONAL INNOVATIONS AND INEQUALITY

The preceding chapters gave the impression that school systems in Asia — and in the context there — tend to increase social and economic inequality. School systems, however, are not always static; they do change, however slowly, and the tendencies of change are made prominent by the flurry of innovations there.[1]

National surveys of innovations undertaken under the auspices of the UNESCO Asian Programme of Educational Innovations for Development (APEID) attest that creative activities in the educational field are legion. The selections made by APEID from those surveys show the far-reaching importance of innovations in the future shape and character of educational systems in Asia.

In the words of the old adage, necessity is the mother of invention. In Asia, as elsewhere, schooling is not the only need that has to be provided for. There has been considerable population growth in the recent past and only dwindling resources are available to cope with a rising tide of school-age children.

In recent years enrolment in the region increased. The proportion of school-age youth attending schools (i.e. the enrolment ratio) has been rising also — which indicates an easing of access to schools. Programmes to reach and serve those who dropped out and those who were not in schools before have been expanding. Some attempts have been made to relate schools to their social environment and to cope with the attendant problems of adjusting to a setting of rural poverty and of influencing parents and other adults towards adopting new modes of thought and lifestyles.

This chapter poses the question whether the innovations and the above-mentioned trends herald the reduction of socio-economic inequality, at least in education. This question is deceptively simple; it is certainly not easy to answer.

Some Reference Points

We recall in this section the use of our two-stage paradigm[2] on the links between education and inequality. During the first stage, the source of

Educational Innovations and Inequality

inequality is in the way learning outcomes are 'distributed' among the pupils, i.e. the distributional patterns of abilities being developed by an educational programme. The next source of inequality is in the second stage, namely from the way the acquired skills are utilised in employment yielding an income. In this discussion we will focus on the first source of inequality, without necessarily ignoring the effects of the second. We direct our attention to the content of educational innovations and its likely impact on learning outcomes of certain kinds, especially among children of the poor in poor countries.

We have already described the classes (and their combination) of the immediate effects of educational activities, i.e. the learning outcomes.[3] We will mention them here only in passing – (a) thinking ability, (b) attitudes and (c) manipulative skills – and recall that in the real world these classes exist not in isolation but in combination. A manipulative skill that has been acquired may be accompanied by a modicum of knowledge and by certain attitudes, whether positive or negative, in relation to some psychological object. The more complex the manipulative skill is, the more it may require higher forms of thinking ability. In some instances, the learning outcomes could be somewhat clear-cut. For example, learning activities in language, mathematics[4] and science could stimulate thinking habits and abilities, while routine repetitive practice could lead to refinement of manipulative skills. And *concientizacion*, one that is advocated by Friere, is likely to arouse a very keen political awareness which, in our typology, would be high in attitudes.

This discussion brings us to the idea that education (i.e. schooling and its variants) is not just a black box. Pedagogical technology exists which can be used to structure the sort of learning outcomes which can be derived from educational inputs and processes. Alternatively, from a given set of inputs and the way it is organised, some structure of the abilities can be reasonably expected. By the same token, information on the educational resources and the curricula used in an innovation would be telling on what is the likely structure of abilities that could be developed. And by knowing the socio-economic origins of the clientele or beneficiary of that educational innovation it is possible to have impressions of the distributional pattern of the learning outcomes.

This distributional pattern, however, gives us only a clue, i.e. that pupils (or other clientele) from different socio-economic origins receive not only a preponderance of certain kinds (types of learning outcomes, not in others) but also some quantum (levels of complexity) of the

150 *Educational Innovations and Inequality*

outcomes. We still need to know, even at a somewhat subjective level, the weights or the values that society or the economy attaches to each of the types of learning outcomes. Given these weights, it would be possible to approximate the total value of a (combination of types) learning outcome. Intuitively we need to know at this point at least the rank order of the three types or dimensions.[5]

The relative importance or value of thinking ability with respect to attitudes or to manipulative skills would depend on the society or economy, and would vary from one organisation or occupation to another. Religious societies would probably be demanding in obedience and piety, traits which are high in attitude content; some of these societies could be stiff both in piety and in abstract contemplation, not only in philosophy but also in science. Business or economic organisations would have a different reward system and stratification; persons who can think and lead are usually placed at the high echelons of the hierarchy, while the doers with their hands (high in manipulative skills) are found on the shopfloor. The differences in pay or rewards are quite often as distant as the floors separating them. These differences are probably not just a matter of practice; they emanate from more profound reasons.

While this differentiation between the values of thinking ability and manipulative skill is easily seen, that of attitudes (and the other two) is difficult to demonstrate. Even by following a technique called paired comparisons most informed readers would probably be indifferent in placing attitudes above or below thinking ability (except perhaps in some religious societies), likewise, above or below manipulative skills, rendering the rank order of the three factors rather artificial.

But the idea of attaching weights (as indicators of value or relative importance, even in a rather subjective sense) is in itself a conceptual advance since it forces the issue of choices in the allocation of educational resources, especially that of learning time. Moreover, and in the intuitive sense, having these weights as numeraire (for prices), the near optimal combination of learning outcomes that could be derived from a given set of input resources and pedagogy could simply be solved as a linear programming problem. And if thinking ability is of much higher value in relation to manipulative skills or attitudes, a linear programme would tend to drive these two abilities out of the solution, suggesting that more and more of the educational resources should be allocated to the production of thinking ability. Or, in the allocation of learning time, more and more of it should be allocated toward the outcomes

Educational Innovations and Inequality

that have much higher value. This view presents a powerful way of assessing the output of educational systems, of educational reforms and, in our discussion, of the innovations in Asian countries.

Classification of Innovations

Following the reference points which we described above, we take particular interest in the domain of the learning outcome,[6] as a means to classify the innovations. There are also other parameters which can be used, namely (a) the clientele or beneficiary, (b) mode of delivery and perhaps (c) costs. We will skip describing again what we meant by the domain of learning outcomes since we have done this already elsewhere.[7]

Target Group. The innovation may be designed for a limited or general target group. It may be addressed to certain age groups such as preschool children, primary school age groups, possibly teenagers who are out of school, or to sex and age groups such as adolescent boys, nursing mothers etc. In some instances, the innovation may be designed for parents of children in school, or simply for all adults in the community.

Mode of Delivery. There is some dispute about the classification of delivery systems, namely the popular trio, i.e. the formal school, non-formal training and the informal learning events.[8] We do not intend to dwell on the distinction between schooling and non-formal training, and between the latter and informal learning; we merely use these terms as adequate descriptors for our purposes.

Cost. Cost is a criterion of obvious special importance for choosing innovations, addressed to the development of highly valued abilities. An innovation which can be introduced at small cost and yet produces a substantial actual or potential effect is naturally a valuable one. Conversely, in order to avoid waste, it is just as important to be able to recognise that some innovations are likely to entail a huge cost with too little foreseeable effect.

All these indicators lead us to the most important consideration of all: *the logic of the innovation.* This criterion permits us to see through the innovation and to determine on the basis of existing knowledge, whether it would work or not, and if it does, whether the likely effects would reduce or exacerbate inequality.

152 *Educational Innovations and Inequality*

Analytic Survey of Innovations

Educational innovations in Asian countries are extremely numerous and the sources of information on them are many. Our major sources, however, are the APEID and informal contacts in many Asian countries.[9]

Asian member states of UNESCO conducted national surveys of educational innovations, which form the basis of the APEID inventory. It does not reproduce all that the member states reported, but consists of selections which may or may not constitute representative samples of the national surveys. However, APEID is an important UNESCO programme, and that organisation can be expected to have exercised care in selecting the innovations worth reporting. In any event, we believe that the innovations recorded in the inventory are the outstanding ones, even though inclusion does not necessarily imply an endorsement by UNESCO that they are the better ones.

Volumes 1 and 2 of the inventory reported a total of 95 innovations, distributed by countries as follows:

Country	*Number of innovations*	*Country*	*Number of innovations*
Afghanistan	1	Rep. of Korea	4
Australia	1	Malaysia	6
Bangladesh	2	Nepal	6
China	3	Pakistan	4
India	12	Philippines	17
Indonesia	8	Singapore	5
Iran	3	Sri Lanka	6
Japan	9	Thailand	8

This distribution does not imply that the numbers indicate which countries are more innovative than others. But it does tell us the sources of the innovations which we are about to assess.

Cognitive Domain

We find a few excellent examples of innovations which are primarily focused on the development of thinking ability. Some of these are: (i) Process Approach and Child Education (PACE), Australia; (ii) Team Teaching, Japan; (iii) Modern Elementary School Mathematics, Philippines; (iv) Individualised Instruction, Philippines; (v) Creative Science Teaching, Japan. Three other innovations which follow similar logic,

Educational Innovations and Inequality   153

i.e. cost reduction in the delivery of existing curricula content, are also worth a mention; they are Project IMPACT (Indonesia and Philippines), Reduced Instructional Time (Thailand) and the In-School, Off-School Approach, or IS-OS (Philippines). All these innovations are of the methods type, i.e. involve the alteration of teaching methods (or the reorganisation of existing methods, including resources) with a view to cultivating the thinking faculty, the aim being either to obtain a better return from existing resources or to spread the resources to cover more pupils without impairing the existing levels of achievement.

(i) PACE in Australia, for example, uses the process approach (one that is derived from Piaget's theories of learning) and compares it with the conventionally enriched curriculum. PACE, also as an experiment, tries to find out whether the process approach promotes or enhances a faster growth in the thinking ability of schoolchildren or 'whether process curricula can induce children to cross stages of intellectual development more rapidly than the ordinary curricula' (EIA No. 57).[10] Besides the cognitive aspects, the process curricula were also intended to develop certain kinds of affective states or attitudes, e.g. moral development, self-concept, attitudes to school, as well as to affect the teacher's teaching style. Evaluation of the innovation revealed that children who were exposed to the process approach demonstrated superior performance in tests of formal operation, in valid inference drawing and in biserial, multiplicative classification.

PACE was conducted as a small-scale, quasi-experimental project in 1972-5 in New South Wales. We have no information, however, on whether it was replicated, expanded or applied on a much wider scale, despite the fact that the project was reported as a success story.

(ii) The Two-Teacher-for-One-Class System in Japan is a variant of the team-teaching approach and is especially designed as a remedial programme for the slow learners, especially those belonging to social groups that are exposed to discrimination. Its purpose is to reduce, if not abolish, discrimination within the school by providing more teachers per class and reducing the class size as well. This sort of 'reverse discrimination' is expected to provide the slow learners with more individualised attention and assistance with their learning difficulties. As a result, once slow learners can be expected to catch up with the rest of the pupils in the same grade before the school term ends.

Again, this innovation was conducted on a trial basis; the experiment was limited to the sixth grade (elementary school), and involved about twelve teachers and 41 to 42 pupils in each class. The experiment was first made in 1974 and repeated in 1975. Evaluation results indicated that while individualised guidance has promoted a better pupil-teacher relationship, it was found extraordinarily difficult to ensure a reasonably high minimum achievement for all pupils.

(iii) Two projects from the Philippines, one on individualised instruction and another on an elementary mathematics curriculum, were developed to improve the achievement levels of pupils in certain subjects (as well as to improve some attitudinal outcomes). The results in the cognitive domain are somewhat obscure. Assessment of the individualised instruction gave the impression that while there was no reduction in the learning of either reading or mathematics, there were significant gains in self-concept and attitudes. At the time of reporting the elementary mathematics curriculum appeared to have brought about some attitudinal changes among school administrators and teachers; information on the effect of the innovations on pupils is still awaiting the analysis of test results.

(iv) A closely related pair of innovations in science teaching were reported from Japan. The first one (EIA No. 63) involves the construction of science kits from waste materials and the second (EIA No. 82) deals with a creative science teaching scheme.

The science kits were assembled from waste material such as jam jars, drinking straws and plastic food containers, which are usually available in quantity. The children were encouraged to bring these materials to school and, with the guidance of teachers, use them in class experiments, ranging from simple to complex assemblies. According to the report, the children make up their own kit and this changes their attitude towards such kits from one of indifference to that of careful maintenance. Children also provide ideas for improving the kits, find new uses for the kit or find new ways to perform experiments.

The other innovation sought 'to ensure the creative teaching of science in every classroom through the creation and use of a standardised teaching plan'. Creation and standardisation appear to be antithetical; yet it is in the latter that an innovation is spread faster by deliberate means. The instructional objectives are analysed by a problem-solving method. The learning process is flow-charted, and achievement is assessed by pupil's self-evaluation as well as by teachers.

The use of 'cost-reducing' and 'learning enrichment' concepts as well as deliberate attempts to improve the intellectual abilities of children in these two innovations are good examples of what schools can do, not only in Japan but also in many other Asian countries.

(v) The following projects, namely Project IMPACT, RIT and IS-OS, are not specific to the cognitive domain. In fact, little information is given concerning the ability domain to which they are primarily directed. But they are innovations in formal schooling, which is mostly directed to the cognitive domain. They are concerned with distributional problems, e.g. the 'search for economical and effective delivery systems for mass primary education' (EIA No. 45).

IMPACT stands for Instructional Management by Parents, Community and Teachers. What used to be called teachers are now called instruction supervisors. Previously they taught classes of 40 or sometimes more; now they manage four to five times that many. The secret lies in learning modules, called 'self-learning kits', and in the assistance provided by community members, parents, pupil peer groups and the less qualified teaching aides.

Pupils progress at their own pace; they can interrupt their studies at any time when necessary, and can resume them at any time too. Achievement levels are indicated by mastery of the modules rather than by classes. The self-learning kits are substitutes for textbooks; a library is now called a 'learning centre', and classrooms are transformed into 'learning centres'. All these innovations are being introduced at two project sites, one in Indonesia and another in the Philippines, which are predominantly rural and relatively depressed areas. More project sites are being opened, certainly in the Philippines and in all probability also in Indonesia as well as in other countries in South-east Asia.

The IS-OS is almost a variant of IMPACT. It makes extensive use of self-learning kits and doubles the teacher-pupil ratio. In-school teaching is continued by 'off-school' learning (in the home) with the self-learning kits, and possibly with the assistance of an adult member of the family who stays at home. In the IS-OS the self-learning kit is a substitute for part of teaching time and relieves the pressure for more classroom space.

Reduced instructional time is still in its early developmental stage, and it is being tried out in Thailand. Its logic lies in the 'careful design and scheduling of instruction',[11] so that a given learning unit can be mastered in a much shorter time than is required by ordinary methods. Thus more children could benefit from existing school facilities and personnel.[12]

There are no firm evaluations yet of RIT, nor of IS-OS. It is suspected that pupils may do less well if they see less of their teachers. The same suspicion was also voiced about IMPACT, but a preliminary comparison of the results of a nationwide examination showed that pupils covered by the IMPACT project performed, if not better, as well as the pupils in conventional classes.

Attitudinal (Affective) Domain

The attitudinal, or affective, domain is rather controversial, especially in relation to the supposed role of schools in fostering attitudes to certain things. One project already mentioned, while directed primarily at cognitive outcomes, recorded significant gains in attitude formation. Another had its first round of attitudinal affects on school administrators and teachers. The expectation is that the effects will rub off onto pupils eventually. Will they?

A prime example of projects in this domain is that on pre-vocational studies (Sri Lanka), including its extensions, namely in-plant training for junior secondary school students, and project work for the higher level. Another is the barrio (village) development school (Philippines). Some components of these innovations are substantially concerned with teaching the manipulative skills, and there are also some components concerned with the development of the thinking faculty. It seems to us, however, that these two components are subordinated to the attitudinal objectives. The pre-vocational study and its extensions are a means of cultivating a love of work, especially of blue-collar work, and of correcting the unduly high job expectations allegedly implanted by schools in school leavers. Likewise, the barrio development school is not devoid of manipulative skill component, nor of the cognitive part, but these are means of reducing the pupils' hopes of higher education and of migrating to urbanising areas, while they are trained to stay on in the village and make it a worthwhile place to live in.

Among many countries in Asia, Sri Lanka seems to have an elaborate, systematic programme for developing proper attitudes towards vocations. In the primary schools, about 20 per cent of the school time is allocated to pre-vocational studies expressly to give pupils 'the opportunity of learning about vocations but not necessarily of acquiring professional skills in them'.[13] The main features of this programme are the following:[14]

Educational Innovations and Inequality 157

(a) it entails the learning of a set of carefully selected psychomotor skills directly related to a vocation;
(b) the manual work that pupils do under a scheme of pre-vocational study is geared towards production;
(c) pre-vocational study places great emphasis on the cognitive study that is necessarily associated with it;
(d) pre-vocational study is intended to bring about far-reaching and significant changes in the affective domain of pupils;
(e) pre-vocational study should help to internalise positive values associated with 'work culture', such as dignity of labour, cleanliness, orderliness, conservation of resources and time, planning self-evaluation, self-discipline and co-operation.

So much about the idealised concept of the programme. In practice, the results are difficult to assess, especially in a field in which assessment is bound to be rather subjective. Attempts to measure the achievement levels in regard to attitudes were made, but the results are not available. On the basis of a questionnaire addressed to teachers, however, it was indicated that in 1972 about 86 per cent of the teachers had reported that their pupils had 'a favourable attitude toward pre-vocational subjects'.[15] This evidence is probably sufficient for many readers but not for others. None the less, that report of a good result is an eye-opener for further evaluation.

In-plant training for junior secondary school students (EIA No. 74) is an extension to the pre-vocational studies programme in Sri Lanka. Its objective is to develop 'basic industrial skills [of] students and instill in them realistic attitudes to the world of work'.[16] Reports on the evaluation of the project seem to reveal that specific as well as aspects of the general objectives which can be assessed immediately were achieved.

Moreover, Sri Lanka has also an innovation called 'project work' for pupils in the senior high schools, which in essence is designed to develop self-confidence among youth through the successful undertaking of worthwhile projects.[17] By undertaking community projects, the students are brought face to face with the real world to confront their book learning with the alternatives before them, especially for the majority (about 85 per cent) who could not proceed to university studies. As a component of the HNCE programme, project work is expected to engender 'skills and correct attitudes' that senior secondary school students 'ought to have'.

Project work is allocated five periods a week of regular school time.

According to the Ministry of Education this allocation is equivalent to about 100 hours per year or 35 six-hour days of the two school years in the senior high school. Students would obviously be spending more time than this, especially after school hours, on community projects. Good marks, including certificates of excellence given for outstanding achievements, ensure that more hours will be spent on project work.

Sri Lanka ensures that pre-vocational and vocational studies are given due importance by pupils and teachers by including these subjects in state examinations for admission to higher education. This is a good step but it runs counter to the very purpose of vocational subjects by reminding the pupils of the reality in Sri Lanka, i.e. that fortune and fame lie not in practical work but in occupations requiring higher studies.

The barrio development school is a post-elementary school programme; like the secondary schools in the Philippines, it requires four years of study (and work); successful completion of the programme does not qualify the pupil for post-secondary education, unless the pupil goes back to high school for about a year, or probably more, and passes a national examination.

Its purpose is down to earth; it is addressed to out-of-school rural youth who decide to stay in the villages and be self-employed there. The programme is based on practical subjects, with a modicum of communication skills, numeracy and civics. Practical work is provided by supervised farming under the guidance of teachers of agriculture. The capital requirements are provided by production loans from rural banks. Within a period of four years, the pupils should accumulate assets and experience that will enable them to become established in farming, if not in other gainful self-employment. This goal appears attractive in a situation of widespread youth unemployment, rural-urban migration and severe rural underdevelopment.

With funding from the World Bank, the barrio development school idea was applied on several sites in Central Luzon, Visayas and Mindanao. A recent visit there gave the authors the impression that (a) there is a serious problem of repayment of the production loans, (b) enrolment is diminishing sharply and (c) there is strong pressure to revise the curiculum to conform with that of the regular high school (presumably in reaction to (b) above). The original barrio development school in Masaya, Laguna, was closed and re-sited in a far more remote village. Moreover, success in the projects did not prevent the former pupils from leaving their villages. All this indicates what happens when attempts are made to solve a predominantly non-educational problem

Educational Innovations and Inequality 159

solely by an educational solution.

There is another striking example in which the school is used to develop favourable attitudes towards the school among adults, so that their children will stay on in school and be prevented from dropping out. This was indexed by APEID as EIA No. 80 and is called 'village community contribution to primary education' (in Indonesia). Its purpose was to develop in the village community a love for school and education so that the community or parents would feel responsible for the education of their children.

The site of the innovation is Les, a village of about 4,000 people, about 36 kilometres from the city of Singaraja; 50 per cent of the people are in the central village and the rest are spread in the estate. According to the inventory, the school drop-out rate in this village was 30 per cent; 'children are not interested in reading [nor] in anything that has to do with reading materials'.

No rigorous evaluation of this project has as yet been made, but after two years of operation, it was reported that new problems seemed to be cropping up and needed to be overcome. Whether or not any progress (e.g. reduction of drop-out rates, increasing interest in reading) has been recorded, nobody knows; but in view of the new problems it would seem to be uncertain.

The assertion that this project is striking brings to mind the various factors which can influence attitudes — in this case, attitudes toward the school. It could be that some school factors are to blame (e.g. inadequate provision of textbooks and other amenities, incompetent teachers); but beyond these, there could be other factors which are formidable, namely the socio-economic circumstances of the village such as severe deprivation which could render the school and schooling of little value to the villagers.

Manipulative Skills

Some of the innovations which we mentioned in connection with attitudes also stressed manipulative skill development. But the latter was merely a means to attitudinal objectives. In fact, one of those which we describe below, i.e. voluntary rural development through education (India, EIA No. 77), appears to have a similar purpose. One feature of this innovation and that of another, namely the job-cum-training scheme (Malaysia, EIA No. 55), is their social welfare character; they are intended for beneficiaries who are left out of the main stream of benefits of public spending.

The Indian example serves the Baraiyas, Patanwadiyas, and other disadvantaged classes. In addition to basic crafts, attitudinal traits such as tolerance, responsibility, discipline and putting service before self, are also taught. The girls are trained in home crafts (e.g. cooking, spinning and weaving, health and hygiene, kitchen gardening, child-rearing). Evaluation of this innovation was in terms of the changes in the outlook of boys and girls receiving the instruction (which were reported to be favourable), rather than in respect of skill development itself.

The Malaysian innovation started with 120 unemployed youths who were recruited to become parking attendants; this was a wise choice between man and machine. The attendants work four hours a day and spend between 8 and 16 hours a week in practical training in subjects such as basic electrical crafts, mechanical craft practice, electrical installation work, building construction, refrigeration and air conditioning, commercial drafting and stenotyping. From 1970 to 1975, 1,137 youths, of whom 1,042 were known to be employed, were trained under the scheme.

Other examples that can be mentioned are the mobile schools (e.g. Mobile Trade Training Schools, Thailand, EIA No. 24; Capiz Mobile School, Philippines, EIA No. 10) which attempt to provide disadvantaged groups with access to skill by non-formal means.

The examples we have make it abundantly clear that manipulative skill training of this nature is usually addressed to children of disadvantaged groups who are (in most cases) squarely among the poor. Whether this training takes place under formal curricula or by non-formal means the target groups appear to be the same.

General Features

Beyond the rather specific learning outcomes there are general features which characterise the trends of innovation in Asia. The interaction between the socio-economic milieu and the transplant models of schools in various parts of this region have brought about not only changes at the margins of school systems but also some transformation of what schools would seem to be. The idea that the entire educational system must also serve the poor and must be made relevant to their circumstances has spurred tendencies towards *vocationalisation* and *ruralisation* of schools. *Non-formal learning* activities were devised to cater to those who did not have access to schools, and conventional programmes such as in literacy have been *functionalised*, i.e. made more practical and useful to the day-to-day lives of the learners. We shall now review these themes before we attempt to assess their impact on

Educational Innovations and Inequality

inequality.

Vocationalisation. The impetus to vocationalisation of secondary school curricula has always been twofold. One of these elements was the awareness of the problem of educated unemployment. For nearly a century commentators have expressed their fear that expansion of academic education at higher levels would inevitably spell increased unemployment for those who received it. The second, and corresponding, element has been the desire to make certain educational courses not only effectively terminal, but clearly seen and expected to be terminal by those taking them. This latter element underlies the streaming that frequently occurs at the beginning or middle of the secondary school cycle into academic and vocational streams on the basis of earlier achievement, generally academic.

Certain countries, such as Thailand, previously attempted to introduce terminal vocational education at an earlier stage: lower secondary vocational schools took in pupils at Grade VIII for a three-year course. These schools have now been all but phased out; they had 1,700 pupils in 1976. The official reason for this step was given as follows:

> In the mid-1960s it became apparent that many vocational skills could not be taught effectively to 14-16 year old children; it was thus decided to gradually abolish vocational education at this level and in its place develop a new system of comprehensive secondary education with a diversified curriculum.[18]

Very similar feelings were voiced by the Indian Education Commission, referring specifically to farming:

> It appears rather unlikely that in a field like agriculture, vocational competence can be given in a period of two or three school years. Farming implies hard work and mature judgement, and the age-group concerned [13+ to 16+] is neither physically nor mentally prepared for this. We also think that overspecialisation at an early age is not at all desirable. Nor are we convinced that the narrowly vocational training is the best use that could be made of school time.[19]

In Sri Lanka, despite serious attempts to change policies in 1951 and 1966, streaming at Grade VIII was not made compulsory, and a common curriculum continues until the end of Grade X.

162 *Educational Innovations and Inequality*

Vocationalisation then, whatever it may have been in certain countries in the past, is now seen as an attempt to head off pupils who have finished lower secondary education from competing for higher education and, in the process, as a means of teaching skills that will secure a steady income. It can therefore be reviewed from those two angles: does it succeed in making terminal courses acceptable, and does it pass on the correct level and kind of skill?

Fairly clearly, vocational streams and vocational schools do not succeed in their heading-off function. For the Philippines, the ILO Comprehensive Employment Strategy Mission reported:

> It is generally conceded that vocational education is unpopular with students and that most of them regard it as a second-best chance to go to college: indeed, 82 per cent of those who finished the vocational track in general high schools in 1968 and 37 per cent of the graduates of special vocational high schools, did subsequently enrol in college.[20]

In Thailand vocational schools in the public sector, or private schools recognised by the Ministry of Education, take in students after Grade X and give a Grade XIII leaving certificate on completion. Academic subjects account for some 40 per cent of school time. The Ministry of Education has explained:

> If vocational secondary education is not to be considered as a dead end form of education, and if it is to continue to attract good students, then it must continue to be considered equivalent to ordinary secondary education in academic terms. Thus the vocational schools have the difficult task of covering in six years (or three years at the upper level) a large proportion of the academic curriculum covered in five years (or two years at the upper level) in academic secondary schools as well as providing the necessary theoretical and practical vocational training.[21]

As a result of this policy, selection for entry to vocational schools is on the basis of academic merit. Furthermore, when it comes to assignment to individual trades, pupils with the highest academic scores have first choice and the others take what is left. Not surprisingly, under these conditions the share of vocational school leavers continuing with further studies frequently reaches 50 per cent, while many observers report that nearly all the pupils want to continue their studies.

One reason why vocational secondary education, despite generally higher costs and longer course time, has failed as a substitute for academic secondary education is precisely that it has also failed to perform its twin task. Vocational secondary education does not guarantee employment. In the Philippines, the ILO Employment Mission concluded: 'There is no evidence to suggest that the graduates of the vocational track find it easier to get jobs than the graduates from the college preparatory track who do not go to college.'[22] The situation in Thailand would appear to be the same.

Most observers have attributed this situation to the very fact that vocational education is being provided in the schools. Schools cannot know where, if anywhere, the job openings will come up, and they cannot reproduce the conditions of outside employment within the school. By all accounts, as the ILO regional team for employment promotion has observed for Thailand,[23] there are always schools that keep in close touch with future employers, accept jobs from industrial clients and have instructors with relevant experience and attitudes. However, those schools would appear to be the exception. Furthermore, they may be fighting a losing battle if the best jobs are reserved for college graduates.

Practical Subjects. As vocational education has become associated with the higher secondary level, so the battlecry for lower secondary or 'middle' grades has become either comprehensive curricula or the introduction of pre-vocational subjects. Both of these lines of approach are intended to make school learning more relevant to employment and more practical, and even, it is hoped, to engender more positive attitudes towards blue-collar occupations. This last was one of the three objectives of the central schools set up in 1941 in Sri Lanka, namely to 'correlate the education imparted to the needs of the locality: to prepare pupils for life and according to their ability and natural aptitudes by creating a love for the village environment and by concentrating on occupations, traditional or otherwise, which could be developed nearer the pupils' homes . . .'[24]

The major difference between comprehensive schools, such as exist in Thailand and previously existed in Laos (the Fa Ngum schools), and pre-vocational studies in Sri Lanka and certain parts of India is that they are optional in the former pair of countries and compulsory in the latter. In Thailand there is a choice not only between comprehensive and other lower secondary schools but also between academic and practical subjects within the schools. This arrangement, however, allows

164 *Educational Innovations and Inequality*

for self-selection by pupils, so that in principle those attending comprehensive schools are those who are interested in practical subjects. That those following practical streams at this lower secondary stage turn to academic streams at the higher secondary stage is no necessary sign of failure of the programme, although the costs per pupil-year for comprehensive schools are more than double those of ordinary lower secondary schools. By concentrating optional practical subjects in special schools, often with a sizeable foreign aid financing component, comprehensive schools should at least be able to offer relevant equipment and specially trained teachers. Countries taking the compulsory route have a different set of problems.

In outlining the following objectives of the Maharashtra programme of work experience, only one, the last, relates to identifying specific employment opportunities. As quoted by the ILO Asian Regional Team for Employment Promotion,[25] the objectives are as follows:

1. To remove the dichotomy between 'cultural' and 'vocational' education, so as to remove social distinctions based on types of educational opportunity.
2. To reduce the existing emphasis on book-learning and to relate academic knowledge to socially oriented productive work.
3. To familiarise pupils with the tools, processes and materials of modern technology, and to impart skills in using them for productive activities.
4. To highlight the direct relationship between modern production and the disciplines of mathematics and science.
5. To enable pupils to develop the habits of work planning, work study, precision, persistence, enterprise and innovation, which are basic for the maintenance of efficiency and progress in all walks of life.
6. To provide opportunities for the pupils to discover their aptitudes and interests through a wide variety of jobs, scientifically planned and executed, so that they may be guided towards a realistic choice of studies and occupational exploration on the completion of the secondary stage.

The ILO team made a number of comments on the performance of this programme. While noting that children welcomed the introduction of this course content, they were very sceptical about the programme's likely success in achieving its last objective. Furthermore, they commented that 'many teachers use teaching methods similar to those used in traditional subjects, and control a substantial part of practical lessons.

Educational Innovations and Inequality

It seems highly doubtful that teachers to be engaged in work experience can obtain desirable teaching techniques and attitudes after one-week training courses.'[26]

Inexperience of teaching staff has been cited as a reason for the gradual introduction of the pre-vocational studies programme in Sri Lanka. This programme, which has the general objective of bringing the content of school work into a closer relation with the world of work, has been introduced for the junior secondary level (Grades VI-IX inclusive). The Sri Lanka pre-vocational programme has been described as follows by the United Nations Economic Commission for Asia and the Far East:[27]

> The Sri Lanka design provides a flexible *modus operandi* for gradually shifting from the present discipline-based, academically oriented school curriculum to one in which the vocational component will be heavy and will increasingly determine the content that has to be taught in the traditional disciplines. This flexibility can be utilized in effecting both the changes in the curriculum desired across the different grades of the school, as well as the rate of change across time at any one level of the school or in any one curriculum. For example, at the beginning, the modules, as they are being evolved, can be taught within the existing curricular framework of disciplines, viz. 'roofs of buildings' under mathematics, 'rubber tapping and manufacture of smoked rubber sheets' under agriculture and 'retail marketing of vegetables' under civics. As the number of modules increases, it would be possible to group them and, from these groups, derive the guidelines to determine the 'academic' part of the curriculum. All the 'process products' of education, such as learning to learn, adaptability, and skills in problem solving, that a traditional curriculum claims to impart can be, of course, equally well cultivated through this content. There is the added advantage that these mental skills will be practised not in academic content areas, which are often several stages removed from the direct experience of the pupil, but in live situations that can be brought within the pupils' experience. The possibility of transfer of learning is thereby greatly enhanced. The pupils will also be able to see the potential scope in some occupations available to them, and receive an initiation, together with some needed concepts and skills. Thus, the school and the community are consciously designed to interact as an integral part of the learning activities of the school.

166 *Educational Innnovations and Inequality*

But despite the many advantages of such a pre-vocational programme there are questions to be raised concerning this, some 20 per cent, allocation of learning time. The problem of whether pre-vocational subjects are to play their part in selecting the future elite or are to be taught at a level which all pupils can enjoy has been posed by Dore, 'If pre-vocational studies become an "easy" subject, then, they may be taken more seriously than if they were not examined at all, but not much more seriously. There will be every reason for making it a difficult subject so that it is taken seriously. This will mean increasing the complexity of the mathematics and general science or economics hung on to the peg of the craft activity, increasing the number of facts to be memorised for reproduction in the examination, increasing, in short, the third, the general education elements, of the three elements listed above. And as this happens pre-vocational studies move further and further away from the craft activity which is their supposed focus; they become instrumentalised as another rung on the ladder into the favoured 10 per cent elite; a means of escaping the necessity of ever having to practise the craft in earnest.'[28]

Functional Literacy Campaigns. Just as lower secondary education is increasingly acquiring a 'practical' tinge, so adult literacy programmes are being transformed into functional literacy programmes. The functional element, which is innovative, can take many forms. At its simplest it is the mere association of literacy training with conceptually unrelated vocational courses, often taught by different instructors under the responsibility of different official agencies. The next level is the 'functionalising' of literacy training, namely the choice of a problem-oriented literacy training curriculum. The question of how to select the 'problem' becomes crucial. Literacy training can revolve around the introduction of new farming techniques, as in certain Indian programmes, or it can attempt to meet the more ambitious criteria specified by UNESCO.[29] These include, in relation to the supposedly 'marginal' illiterate population, insertion into the milieu, mastery of the milieu and transformation of the milieu. These last two objectives correspond closely to those of other programmes which are not explicitly literacy oriented, such as the New Delhi National Labour Institute's rural labour camps for landless labourers and sharecroppers (which have none the less identified night schools as a major need). Such programmes accept that the rural poor and illiterate are of the milieu but that they have no mastery over it and should be encouraged to transform it.

Its objectives are not necessarily the only innovative aspects of a functional literacy programme. First, a particular occupational group can be selected and its literacy curriculum related to that group: thus under the functional literacy drive in Iran 28 different programmes were adjusted to the work problems of various adult groups. Secondly, innovative teaching procedures can be used not only in the integration of work and literacy activities but also, for example, in teaching arithmetic through other forms of technical training. Thirdly, under such programmes an attempt can be made to escape from classroom-oriented pupil-teacher relationships into peer group discussion, group activities and communally assessed efforts.

A first point of interest in relation to the success of functional literacy programmes is their high drop-out rate. In Iran this was probably as high as 60 per cent for the two-year cycle programme.[30] This rather suggests that however relevant and well prepared a functional literacy programme may be, it is never going to be a vehicle for achieving mass literacy. High drop-out rates were experienced despite a high level of initial enthusiasm for the programmes: however, for those who stayed the course, a programme of about 300 hours is considered to have ensured the same level of basic training as a five-year primary-school cycle.

In addition to success in achieving the literacy objectives of functional literacy programmes, experience in Iran and India does suggest that direct economic objectives were also achieved. In Jaipur and Lucknow functional literacy gave rise to 'significantly increased desire for technical information and to significantly intensified behaviour designed to satisfy that desire'.[31] In Iran the functional literacy programme was considered to have had positive results on family planning. In both countries indicators of personal wealth and income, i.e. possession of consumer goods, opening bank accounts, suggest that successful participants in functional literacy programmes were economically successful. However, while participants might in this way begin to learn the rules of the game in their own milieu, they would not appear to have begun to transform it.

A point emerging from the operation of functional literacy programmes in Iran was that overspecificity in relation to vocational curricula is no advantage. The most popular curricula in Iran were fairly general, and oriented towards household problems, they were also followed by many teenage children. In addition it became apparent that older workers are interested in occupational problems of a more general nature. Thus general agricultural curricula were also followed by industrial workers. But functional literacy programmes can be seen to have considerable problems. The very general use of primary school teachers as instructors is likely to lead to the use of inappropriate teaching methods and an overemphasis on the academic side of functional literacy. Interaction of literacy and strictly vocational training means involving at least two government agencies, all the way from the highest to the lowest level. More general functional literacy programmes require considerable work on designing a problem-oriented curriculum which participants will accept as useful and be willing to follow for a couple of years. Finally there must be follow-up. In this case follow-up is a matter not only of providing reading materials but also of creating the conditions in which the new-found literacy is to be used. Such conditions may include the supply of fertiliser, but they may also include the creation of new institutional forms and procedures in a wider field.

Ruralisation. Ruralisation can be presented as an extreme manifestation of the concerns behind the initiation of practical studies. It poses the question, is there not a form of primary education which will have positive effects on the attitude of school leavers towards village life and furthermore serve to bring about not only attitudinal changes among villagers but practical changes within the village? The introduction of a rural emphasis in education can be regarded as a means of tying rural children to the village by adapting the school curricula to village needs in such a way that urban employers will see rural education as second-best education. This interpretation and objective are violently rejected in countries (such as Cameroon, to take a non-Asian example) where ruralisation is an aim of policy. In fact, in that country official reports stress that 'the ruralised school should at the same time prepare the best pupils to pursue their studies, and the remaining bulk of pupils to integrate into working life, using the same curricula and methods in both town and country'.[32]

On this interpretation 'ruralisation' does not mean a different curriculum for rural and urban schools; nor, very clearly, does it mean closing all avenues of continued education. What then are its basic features? The basic element seems to be a close integration of the school into the community by introducing rural work activities into the curriculum, teaching basic abilities through environmental studies and having the school teacher assume an 'animating' role in the community. In this sense ruralisation is perhaps the answer to a very specific situation in time and space, one in which even primary education has an elitist element, probably relying on a foreign language for teaching, and

Educational Innovations and Inequality

in which primary school teachers are cut off from their local community. 'Ruralisation' does not require the primary school teachers to be agricultural or health technicians, but it would seem to require them to assume some responsibility as intermediaries or organisers for the supply of agricultural or health services. In more sophisticated communities they would not be able to play such a role even if they wanted to.

The introduction of rural work activities into the primary curriculum may mean all sorts of things: it can be presented as a means of making the school a model for the village because the school has properly constructed cowsheds or latrines. But no definitive comment can be made unless one knows how much time is to be allocated to such activities and how they are to contribute to the selection of children for secondary education. The risk that such activities as keeping a few chickens or growing vegetables may have little or no effect on children's attitudes or village knowledge is very great. It is furthermore in general recognised that work activities for children in the fifth and sixth primary grades cannot be a form of vocational training, as was stated by the Indian Education Commission quoted earlier. Of course, if the purpose of ruralisation were to be that performance in rural work activities, or the accumulation of knowledge through such work experience, was to become the means of selection for further studies, at the expense of the development of mental abilities, it would have serious and far-reaching consequences, but it is not presented in that way.

What is left of the concept of ruralisation, if it makes no claims to anything beyond the development of recognised abilities, such as the ability to think, to act and to learn? The residue is, in fact, the development of a new curriculum of environmental studies which is probably not unlike certain elements of pre-vocational studies in Sri Lanka. If it is not this, then it would seem to be the improvement of existing curricula, to make them more interesting and to make use of relevant and familiar examples in teaching. In this respect different countries have different degrees of improved or relevant curricula; most countries, however, are suffering from similar educational problems.

Summary

And so we pose the question again: will the innovations lead to a reduction of inequalities?

The foregoing survey of innovations leaves us with the impression that very few innovations were focused on learning outcomes as such; they were concerned with wider socio-economic objectives; they were valiant attempts to solve pressing social problems such as youth unemployment, rural-urban migration, poor nutrition and health and bad living conditions, and to expand the services of the schools beyond their immediate walls. These problems are quite demanding of the schools' resources, while their reallocation of pupils' learning time gives unclear results and is of uncertain effectiveness.

Some innovations which have clearly high cognitive content were those taking place in the formal schools, institutions that are attended mostly by the fortunate few. Efforts to introduce new pedagogical methods into the classrooms were made in rural areas and in schools located in depressed sections of urban areas, and were intended to increase the number of pupils who could be served by existing facilities and resources. However, they stopped short of redressing the rather low learning levels achieved by the children of the underprivileged. As for the sporadic remedial attempts to help slow learners, they led to significant gains in attitude development rather than in thinking abilities.

Innovations that extend the services of schools to rural areas and the disadvantaged groups were marked by an emphasis on manipulative skill development and on the formation of certain attitudes (e.g. the reduction, if not repression, of unduly high expectations about white-collar jobs); these two types of learning outcomes are usually regarded as being of less economic value than thinking ability. In a sense this observation points out a likely effect of vocationalisation and its extension (e.g. ruralisation) of educational programmes, namely that they would tend to maintain, if not worsen, the position of the already disadvantaged. As it were, the innovations, like the school systems and the social milieu from which they emerged, tend to reproduce the existing rather inequitable social order.

We are aware that our criticisms of vocationalisation and ruralisation may themselves be misunderstood. Some observers will no doubt propose that since many children of the poor will take up routine manual jobs they should be taught to do such tasks well at an early age. Our criticism is not that the poor will not or do not need manipulative skills. Nor is the sole reason for our criticism that stress on teaching manipulative skills will deny equality of opportunity to the children of the poor, although it will have that effect. We also believe that teaching manipulative skills at the expense of cognitive skills is shortsighted and

Educational Innovations and Inequality

wasteful. It is not experience with a particular set of manipulative skills which is most useful to the children of the poor but the ability to absorb new skills and to adjust the old ones. This ability is itself more cognitive than manipulative.

Notes

1. For a working definition of an educational innovation, see A.M. Huberman, *Understanding Change in Education: An Introduction* (Paris, UNESCO, IBE, 1973).

2. See also M.D. Leonor Jr, *Education and Productivity: Some Evidence and Implications*, mimeographed World Employment Programme research working paper (restricted) (Geneva, ILO, 1976).

3. See Chapter I of the present study.

4. Literacy and numeracy are classifiable under thinking ability, viz. the ability to decode and encode symbols from facts and facts back to symbols.

5. These types or dimensions were referred to earlier, p. 17.

6. We refer to the domains of the abilities, namely (a) cognitive domain (thinking ability), (b) affective domain (attitudes) and (c) psychomotor domain (manipulative skills).

7. See note 1.

8. For formal descriptions of classification, see Philip H. Coombs et al., *New Paths to Learning for Rural Children and Youth* (New York, International Council for Educational Development, 1973), pp. 10ff.

9. We should also mention the series of publications on Experiments and Innovations in Education covering a much wider region published by the International Bureau of Education, UNESCO.

10. EIA means Educational Innovations in Asia, and the number following it refers to the entry in the APEID Inventory.

11. Nuanchan Potar, 'Project RIT (Reduced Instructional Time)', *Innotech Journal* (March 1977), pp. 29-30.

12. We do not know whether these favourable test results can be maintained.

13. See W. Diyasena, *Pre-vocational Education in Sri Lanka* (Paris, The UNESCO Press, 1976), p. 6.

14. Ibid., pp. 6f.

15. Ibid., p. 41.

16. Ibid.

17. See *HNCE Project Work: A Guide to Teachers* (Colombo, Ministry of Education, 1976), p. 6.

18. Ministry of Education, *Education in Thailand* (1971).

19. *Report of the Education Commission* (New Delhi, 1966), para 14.46.

20. ILO, *Sharing in Development: A Programme of Employment, Equity and Growth for the Philippines* (Geneva, ILO, 1974), pp. 310-20, quoting the report of a Presidential Commission to Survey Philippine Education.

21. Ministry of Education, *Education in Thailand*.

22. ILO, *Sharing in Development*, p. 322.

23. ILO Asian Regional Team for Employment Promotion, *Training for Employment in Thailand* (Bangkok, 1974).

24. J.E. Jayasuriya, *Education in Ceylon before and after Independence* (Colombo, 1969), cited in R. Dore, *Pre-vocational Studies – a Comment on*

Recent Developments in Ceylonese Education, Vol. 2, No. 2 (Marga, Colombo, 1973).

25. ILO Asian Regional Team for Employment Promotion, *Generating Employment for the Educated in India* (Bangkok, 1973), citing State Institute of Education, Maharashtra, *Maharashtra Action Research Project in Occupational Education and Training*.

26. Ibid.

27. Economic Commission for Asia and the Far East, *Economic Survey of Asia and the Far East 1973, Part 1, Education and Employment*.

28. Dore, *Pre-vocational Studies*.

29. See UNESCO: UNDP, 'The Experimental World Literacy Programme, A Critical Assessment' (Paris, 1976).

30. Ibid. Substantial drop-out rates were reported for many countries participating in the programme.

31. Ibid., p. 177.

32. Quoted in R. Lallez, *An Experiment in the Ruralisation of Education, IPAR and the Cameroonian Reform* (Paris, The UNESCO Press, 1974).

9 SUMMARY, CONCLUSIONS AND RECOMMENDATIONS

Summary

In this final chapter it is necessary to reiterate and to link together the major points of the preceding chapters. We began by stating our unwillingness to accept the proposition that educational expansion would have beneficial effects on Asian income distribution. We also expressed our doubt that 'right' and 'wrong' kinds of education exist, at least in terms of a dichotomy between 'academic education' and 'vocational training'. From the beginning we stressed that the connection between education and income distribution must be properly seen in terms of two stages. At the first stage household income and other household background factors (of the type brought out in Chapter 6 and for which the father's occupation is used as a proxy in Chapter 5) are connected with the educational achievement of the children. At the second stage the circle is completed as children's educational achievement is connected with their later position within the labour force. On balance we felt that this constantly repeating two-stage process produced few intergenerational changes.

In Chapter 1 we noted first some dilemmas in adopting equality as an objective in the field of education: equal inputs are unlikely to produce equal results. Because we regard education as the process of ability creation, we have tended, in Chapters 4 and 5 in particular, to view equality in education as the achievement of equal levels of ability creation. However, there are different kinds of abilities — broadly cognitive or mental ability, attitudes and aspirations (affective states) and psychomotor or manipulative skills. Furthermore, different in-school learning processes can have different effects on the development of those abilities. Despite the scope for flexibility in the organisation of school time and school activities, however, researchers have generally found that the socio-economic background of pupils is the major determinant of their educational achievement, although schooling assumes greater importance when learning opportunities at home are meagre.

In Chapter 1 we also made the point that jobs requiring mental skills or highly developed cognitive abilities are universally better rewarded, in pay and status, than jobs requiring largely manual and psychomotor

174 Summary, Conclusions and Recommendations

skills. Above all 'learning to learn', development of the capacity to adjust to and benefit from changing situations, requires the development of cognitive and, perhaps, affective abilities.

In Chapter 2 we shifted our focus away from the educational process towards education and employment relationships. We first noted the widespread evidence that greater educational investment in a person is generally reflected in his or her higher earnings. Furthermore, education interacts with age, generally in such a way that additional years of age have a greater effect on earnings for highly educated workers than for those who are less highly educated. We went on to suggest that it may be the occupational structure of an economy which determines both the structure of output of the educational system and the pattern of income distribution. Inequality of educational achievement would then be built into the labour market structure, and would be a necessary condition for the labour market to function normally. The capability of the educational system to ensure equality of educational achievement would accordingly be limited. In describing the interaction of education and employment we noted the major role which the government plays as an employer in Asia. Generally governments have an inflexible attitude towards wage differentials. As a result the job competition model of school leavers queuing up for jobs to become vacant (or to be created), with consequent unemployment, is, for the educated, a better description of labour market behaviour than the possibility of wage competition between job aspirants.

Following on from the preceding chapter, Chapter 3 investigated the effect of educational expansion on the labour market, mainly in the Philippines and Sri Lanka. The chapter first discussed where, in the labour market, the additional years of education produced have been used. In fact in both countries we found, largely on the basis of data relating to the 1960s, that most educational investment was ultimately finding its way into the occupations which already had the highest levels of education. The share of educational investment devoted to the agricultural labour force either fell or remained constant. Our analysis suggests that 'educational inflation' is rampant in clerical and higher-level occupations, and can be expected to continue. Much of the extra output of the educational system is used up in fuelling this inflation. The chapter went on to look at average incomes and their distribution by occupation and by level of education. There is no common pattern in the distribution of income, as measured by Gini coefficients, by education level. If the unemployed are taken into account as zero income receivers, this income distribution naturally becomes more unequal. In both countries the distribution of years of education within any occupational group has generally narrowed. However, the distribution of income within occupational groups is generally more equal than within educational groups. The conclusion reached in this chapter was that the overall distribution of work incomes probably owes much more to the distribution of occupations and to factors operating on occupational income independently of educational level, than to the distribution of education.

In Chapter 4 we switched the focus of our analysis away from the interaction of employment and income and back to the generation of inequality in education. We compared educational achievement, in terms of scores from a test of reading comprehension, for schoolchildren of comparable age or grade from rich and poor countries. In principle educational inputs were broadly equal, but outputs were not. In this example not only were the average scores of the industrialised countries participating far higher than those of the developing countries (India, Iran and Chile), but the variation in their results was also far lower. Furthermore, test scores in the industrialised countries seemed to vary less as the children grew older. This was not so in the poorer countries. The gap between the two sets of countries in fact increased with the age of the children.

The hypothesis of Chapter 5 was that the pattern of inequality in educational achievement shown internationally in Chapter 4 would be repeated at the national level, if household occupational status was used as the differentiating factor. This analysis was made for three countries, India, Iran and Thailand, using the results of tests intended to probe acquisition of functional information, comprehension, application of information learned and the operation of higher mental processes. It had been found that in industrialised countries differences in performance on these tests between children from different occupational household backgrounds were highly significant, with the advantages of children from higher occupational households increasing in line with the complexity of the mental process being tested; differences diminished somewhat with age, presumably as a result of selection processes within the education system. In general the same pattern occurs in the developing countries examined, despite the small number of observations in certain categories: test performances seem to reveal that, on average, children of labourers and similar occupations have a less developed thinking faculty than children of members of the professions or of management. This finding would indicate that while the school certificates obtained or the number of years of schooling may be equal,

176 Summary, Conclusions and Recommendations

the pupils have no semblance of equality in thinking ability.

Chapter 5 paved the way for a national analysis, in Chapter 6, of differential school attendance, test scores and university enrolment in the Philippines. In this case the results of the national college entrance examination, of Project SOUTELE (survey of outcomes of elementary education) and of applications for admission to the University of the Philippines were examined in relation to background characteristics of the pupils' households. For the college entrance examination a number of variables were associated with lower scores; they included the level of schooling and of income of parents, a rural background and the type of school attended. Our analysis of data from Project SOUTELE shows that the same factors appear to be operative at the primary-school level. Indeed, such factors are probably at work even before the children set foot in school. At the level of higher education we found that the probability of access to the high-status University of the Philippines is highly biased towards high-income groups. This impressive array of evidence from the Philippines certainly suggests that although the early display of talent and assiduity may partly compensate for low household incomes, the limiting effects of low incomes on children's educational achievement are formidable. Such evidence inevitably suggests that there will be a continuation of the intergenerational reproduction of poverty.

In Chapter 7 we continued this line of analysis at the national level, bringing in evidence for additional countries — India, Sri Lanka and Thailand. For these countries we do not have the test scores that were available for the Philippines, so that our argument is based mainly on school attendance. Even using this variable (which, as we have seen, is probably less sensitive to socio-economic background than are test scores), we find very considerable variation according to occupation, income group, region and, for India, caste. For Sri Lanka we find, for example, that the children of the poor enter school relatively late and move more slowly through the school system. In both India and Sri Lanka it seems very likely that the poorest sections of the population, generally landless labourers in rural areas and some slum dwellers, frequently see little possibility of social mobility for their children through education. Without firm encouragement and in the face of uninteresting education of low quality, the children drop out. In this chapter we also noted that the fast rate of expansion of secondary education, before full enrolment has been achieved at the primary level, reflects a demand from certain parents and politicians, with the support of educational administrators.

Summary, Conclusions and Recommendations 177

In Chapter 8 we looked at recent innovations in educational systems in the light of our knowledge first that cognitive abilities are those best rewarded by the labour market (through access to higher occupations) and secondly that testing the development of mental abilities is likely to separate children along lines determined by household background factors. We found that many innovations which were aimed at extending the services of schools to poorer groups placed most stress on less rewarded manipulative skills. Furthermore, such innovations were often aimed precisely at reducing levels of aspiration for intergenerational social mobility. Conversely, other innovations aimed at introducing familiarity with manual work threaten to be self-defeating by relying on the development of cognitive elements in such practical subjects as a necessary selection step on the educational ladder. But our general impression is that few innovations were focused where they should be, on improving the educational achievements of children from poorer socio-economic groups. More frequently, innovations were attempts to solve wider socio-economic problems such as youth unemployment, which are beyond the schools' control. Such innovations are apt to reallocate pupils' learning time to activities with unclear results and uncertain effectiveness.

In this connection we can once more refer back to our introductory doubts on the benefits of educational expansion for income distribution. We have noted the very prevalent inequality in educational results and achievements in Asia. We have seen also the extent of educational inflation and the pressures generated through the labour market which work towards inequality, at least in the number of years of education completed, not to mention other respects. Educational expansion, meaning the provision of more inputs to the education system, is likely to be used and laid claim to primarily by groups that are already influential, in order to compete in this inflationary process. Secondly, it is almost impossible that this expansion will ever bring about equality in educational achievements which it is not intended to do. The links are very strong between academic success and high levels of educational achievement, the development of mental ability and access to better-paid jobs and occupations. Developing other types of ability, especially for the poor, leaves the field of competition in mental abilities free for the non-poor. Given the present pattern of reward structures in the labour market and given the need for educational systems to respond to this pattern, educational expansion cannot be expected to improve income distribution in any significant fashion.

Conclusions and Recommendations

Behind our analysis in the earlier chapters stand certain assumptions about the task of school systems. We assume that those systems exist in order to develop abilities, through a learning process which differs in kind from that which operates in the home, at play or, in later life, at the place of work. Thus schools are means of developing a specific set of abilities among children and young people. Because of this function of developing ability, schools are increasingly given a 'labelling' function as well, and the results of school testing of developed abilities become authoritative and determining, even in later life. Schools do not, of course, develop abilities in a vacuum. They must build on home background factors and they must work in conjunction with other out-of-school factors. We have found that the abilities of the poor are developed to a lower level even at school. This finding implies a less successful schooling experience, a less supportive home background and a less relevant range of out-of-school activities. Furthermore, the poor are much less likely to be in school, to have started school (or started at a favourable age), to have remained at school for the normal period or to have succeeded in school. There is thus inequality both in results and in opportunity; and the joint effects of inequality in those two respects will widen the disparities between the rich and poor.

To understand how a school system can contribute towards eradicating the inequalities in results and opportunity we have to realise first why they occur and secondly how such inequalities will later determine other inequalities in earnings and incomes. These two sets of inequalities are closely linked and account for the intergenerational linkages and the different perceptions that various social and occupational groups (not necessarily the rich and the poor as such) may have of the relevance and utility of education for their children. We have seen that groups with pessimistic perceptions of their chances for social mobility may give a lower rating to the value of education. Conversely, education has been used by more ambitious and otherwise well-supported groups as a direct aid to social mobility.

The major reason for the existence and persistence of inequalities in educational access and outputs may be summarised as a case of 'multiple deprivation'. This is intended as a blanket expression to cover low levels of physical resources and their consequences, low levels of ambition and hope, perhaps a predominance of fear and superstition, low levels of communication, knowledge and information and absence of local influence. Naturally all these elements are linked together

Summary, Conclusions and Recommendations

through inadequate employment opportunities, inadequate nutrition, insecurity, positive value of child labour, expense of books, absence of reading materials at home and poor employment prospects. Such factors are going to determine ability to go to school, regularity of attendance in school, to some extent interest in school (in-school factors must be important here) and ability to benefit by school teaching and by following school curricula. No one denies that in rare cases the stranglehold of these factors can be broken, but their concerted influence is extremely strong.

The role of schools in promoting equality is influenced not only by multiple deprivation but also by the ranking of developed abilities in the labour market generally. Schools develop certain kinds of abilities and spend more time and effort developing certain abilities, namely higher mental abilities, than others, namely manual dexterity. These abilities command different sets of rewards in the labour market. As economies become more homogeneous, the ranking of abilities and rewards becomes more fixed. Only the ownership of physical capital is likely to change the ranking although, even there, different sets of abilities will have different effects on the profitability with which physical capital is managed. The general rule applies that possession of certain mental abilities qualifies job-seekers for 'higher' occupation jobs while possession of cruder manual abilities leads only to more lowly occupations. Since reward structures appear to be reflections of occupational structures in almost all societies, we find that the children of the rich are more likely than the children of the poor to end their school days in possession of the well-rewarded type of abilities.

It is theoretically conceivable that a society could develop with a different reward structure and a different hierarchical ranking of abilities and earnings. Though conceivable, such a change is highly improbable. The labour market may succeed in making marginal changes as manual labour gradually becomes scarcer and the technological basis of economic production changes. But for most Asian developing countries no significant changes of this nature can be expected for the next fifty years at least.

In view of the limitations imposed by these two factors — multiple deprivation and the ability-earnings structure — there is little that schools can achieve. They cannot be expected to bring about significantly greater income equality. As we shall discuss below, there are beneficial changes which can be made in school systems and which should achieve at the least greater equality of opportunity; furthermore, the people who run the schools should become aware of some of the conservative implications of seeming innovations. But schools cannot change the ranking of earnings and abilities: far from it, schools reflect market valuations of different kinds of abilities in the way they operate, their division of learning time, their testing procedures and their selection of their own personnel.

It must be realised that the objective of educational systems to produce a set of basic abilities for everyone is almost beyond reach unless multiple deprivation is overcome by action over a broad field including food availability, income security, debt redemption, a healthy environment and other components of better living. Thus all these things must go forward together, educational changes hand in hand with general socio-economic changes. Educational changes, made in order to develop basic abilities, must be an integral part of any policy of social change. The educational changes required are obviously not those which are generally made under the heading of innovation, since such changes may worsen the relative situation of the poor, but changes which require redistribution of resources towards the poor.

In this context the socio-economic changes required are not just those which produce wide attainment of minimum levels. Policies which aim to bring everyone up to a minimum imply a free-for-all above the minimum. Such a free-for-all in turn implies freedom to develop new techniques, innovations which will benefit more those who pass beyond the minimum than those who just reach it. Such minima will make only marginal inroads on the existing inequality, and have built-in tendencies towards increasing inequality. The necessary strategy for education, and for other sectors, needs to be one which achieves the universal minimum by means of other changes. The other changes are those that, even if they cannot guarantee built-in tendencies towards equality, are at least free from most dangers of the opposite. This is as true for education as it is for, say, agricultural production (and the development of new agricultural practices) or industrial production (and access to credit and new technology). Clearly it is not easy to accomplish changes of that nature. Particularly in education there is no tide which can be taken at the flood, no series of interlocking, mutually reinforcing measures inexorably leading to greater equality through popular awareness and participation and government response. There may be such trends in certain forms of development, capitalist and other, but they are hard to initiate.

We have mentioned the possibility of achieving greater equality of opportunity. No doubt school systems can be restructured in ways that will help; yet equality of educational opportunity, which also requires corresponding action to overcome many of the characteristics of multiple deprivation, may have little effect on the structure of earnings if the latter is predominantly determined by social class. Greater income equality can possibly follow from two different courses of action. The first is a wider distribution of the better-paying jobs among members of different social classes. As a result, the savings which are possible from the higher incomes may be more widely spread and inherited by a large number of families. Thus the inequality of unearned, as opposed to earned, income may diminish.

The second course stems from the fact that higher levels of education for people in generally lower-status occupations may increase their bargaining power and reduce the inequality in earned incomes. As we have seen, little progress has been made towards the preliminary educational objective and the inequality of educational investment in the labour force has hardly diminished in recent years, at least in the Philippines and Sri Lanka. But if objectives other than a reduction in measured income inequality are to be adopted as, of course, they are by most governments, such as universal schooling to a certain level, then basic equality of opportunity becomes essential. In Asian circumstances, the achievement of this equality of opportunity requires a redirection of resources towards the parts of school systems that are the only ones usually open to the poor.

What kinds of action would be required for this kind of equality in school systems to be achieved through a redistribution of internal resources, and how feasible are such changes? The required changes would depend on circumstances. They can range from adequate buildings to financial inducements to the parents to send their children to school, and, indeed, inducements to the parents themselves to provide a more supportive home background. Thus it would first have to be decided how the school system would interact with other agencies and programmes in overcoming the obstacles of multiple deprivation. It should be clear that there is no measured level of inputs which will at some stage be 'adequate' to ensure equality of opportunity and the provision of a basic education. Rather it must always be a question of balance among the resources society has allocated for education. The extent of financial commitment towards achieving equality of opportunity will need to be decided in relation to that balance. Specified ratios of pupils to teachers with certain qualifications, with so many books and the use of so many facilities, will not overcome educational deprivation if home background factors are not simultaneously allowed for. As we have repeatedly stressed, the achievement of 'decent' educational facilities at, for example, the primary level may well be compatible with considerable inequality at higher levels. Furthermore, 'decent' facilities will soon become 'inadequate' if innovations and other measures to improve technical efficiency are introduced at another level without regard for the need to preserve a certain balance overall. In general, input indicators are not sufficient in this context; output indicators of abilities developed are needed, and even they will need to be revised as time goes by.

But it can certainly be asked how feasible is a redirection of educational resources, not just towards the provision of basic education for all the children of the poor (which would quickly be subsumed by most governments under a target of, say, 95 per cent enrolment in primary schools) but of equal education and equal educational chances for the poor? Again, this becomes an open question. The likelihood of action bearing simultaneously on pupils' in-school and out-of-school environments is very slight. But in any event various factors make the pattern of emphasis of an educational system difficult to change. Job scarcity and the schools' role in certification are undeniable in most Asian developing countries, and they are major stumbling blocks to any significant change. In fact they are the determinants of a number of innovations in educational systems which will take those systems further from any role of inducing equality. School systems are, after all, part and parcel of the societies in which they exist, and the scope of school administrators for action contrary to the expressed wishes of those societies is very slight. Furthermore, schooling is a subject very much in the public eye; the foundation and expansion of schools are governed by the play of forces in the local political arena. And, in the simplest terms, the maintenance or upgrading of schools will not rebound as much to a politician's credit, and will not attract as many votes, as building a completely new school.

It is the nature of the role of the education system within society which explains why the school system cannot follow another short cut towards greater equality in education. This would be to test and put more time and other resources into developing a set of abilities which the poor are likely to be as successful in mastering as the rich, or even more so. These abilities would not be the mental abilities which are the objectives of current schooling but others such as motivation, loyalty, capacity for effort or certain simple vocational skills. As we have mentioned in discussing innovations, the development of such abilities does have a place in certain school curricula, and there are schools of thought which would have them figure more prominently. Where they are included, however, far less weight is attached to them than to the development of mental skills, simply because society places a higher premium on the latter. Thus, while the schools may well be able to develop abilities at which the poor would shine, there is no guarantee that these abilities would be found worth rewarding in any economy. Furthermore, time spent on generating such abilities reduces the time and resources available for generating and developing the abilities which parents, particularly more influential parents, know are essential for their children in a competitive world.

Related to this question of developing a different set of abilities is that of different forms of examinations. Many criticisms of examination systems in developing countries concentrate on their excessive reliance on testing knowledge achieved through rote learning, largely because teachers are poorly trained. (Under-trained teachers feel more confident in teaching through a repetition of facts, and support examination systems which evaluate children's progress by counting the facts their pupils have correctly absorbed.) Aptitude testing has been suggested as an improvement on conventional examinations because it allows rote learning to be avoided and because aptitude tests 'can be more discriminating in the kinds of ability they test, separating verbal ability from mathematical reasoning ability, mechanical aptitude from artistic aptitude and so on'.[1]

Such proposals have been criticised for two main reasons. First, if they are to be successfully applied, more imaginative teaching is required, and, as Blaug puts it, 'if we are going to abolish examinations and replace them with aptitude tests, the worst place to start is in the less developed countries'.[2] Secondly, while there are many forms of aptitude testing, none would appear to be capable of abstracting, from the home background, variables and abilities developed by the school. Indeed, results of aptitude tests would seem to be frequently well correlated with those of conventional examinations. Shifting to aptitude testing then, if that were a real possibility, might improve the content of the school curriculum, but it is not at all obvious that it would have beneficial distributional consequences. Indeed, there is a suspicion that in many forms of aptitude testing the children of the rich would be even more likely to out-perform the children of the poor.

Aptitude testing is not one of the current innovations being tried out in Asia. As we mentioned in the summary of Chapter 8, many of these innovations would appear to constitute attempts to use the education system to change the whole substance and structure of the economy. It is true that educationists have often stood accused of the

184 *Summary, Conclusions and Recommendations*

attitude 'we turn out school graduates, someone else must find jobs for them'; and indeed educationists can be convicted of conniving at the very least in the unnecessary (and inequitable) inflation of educational qualifications. The spirit of the above accusation, like that of the response of educational planners and administrators, has been that changing attitudes towards the acceptance of socially undervalued forms of employment and self-employment were the key to social and economic change: success in changing attitudes would be half the battle won. However, we know that such success is neither likely nor enduring, if the reward structure is unfavourable. Clearly we are sceptical about some claims. For example, attempts to change attitudes by allocating more resources to pre-vocational education will hardly affect the situation, especially for children who fail to complete primary education, and indeed may result in a mistaken redirection of time, attention and money. Secondly, so long as the hierarchical ranking of jobs and earnings remains there will be competition for them in which school variables and tested abilities will play a major part. Stress on adopting different attitudes will be almost certainly self-defeating and is least likely to be accepted by the children whose home background is in any event closest to that of existing holders of the most coveted jobs.

It is not by action along such lines that we expect the multiple deprivation discussed earlier to be defeated. Changes in school systems will be needed, but they must be accompanied by changes in other respects, and cannot be substitutes for such other changes. Can we then briefly specify which abilities school systems should aim to develop, given other changes in the economy as part of a comprehensive plan to overcome deprivation?

To raise this question is to confront orthodox ideas, including the fashions and fancies which tend to become part of the recent orthodoxy, on what schools should do (and not do) and on the choices regarding the use of resources allocated to schools. To expect a specific answer is to beg the question of the specific setting in which a school system is deeply embedded. On the other hand, a universal answer is at best incomplete and could be no more than a general guideline until the unknowns are charted. Yet to raise the question is already to make a good start in the quest for answers applicable in specific socio-economic conditions, although such answers will not be simple or easy to find.

What we can do at this stage is to offer clues to some potential answers, without ruling out the possibility that there may be other

Summary, Conclusions and Recommendations

equally useful clues. Within the confines of an economic perspective, the likely answer lies in the labour market, i.e. the abilities that are well rewarded.[3] Here we recall earlier suggestions (Hartog's 'capability variable', Lydall's 'I and D factors', Tinbergen's 'leadership and independence', Welch's 'allocative ability' and Schultz's 'ability to deal with disequilibria') and point out the primary role of schools in laying the foundation for the development of these highly complex abilities. Multiple deprivation disables children; many schools exacerbate this disability even more by allocating precious learning time to tasks unconnected with the development and strengthening of those basic abilities. Later, the cruelly unequal effects of this disability begin to bite when the children, already grown up, enter the labour market or go to work. If they are to contribute towards the reduction of economic inequality, schools must be used in a positive sense to redress this disability in concert with other socio-economic measures. This means that equality of opportunity must be seen to be promoted by the axioms of 'reverse discrimination', and by compensatory measures that will truly serve the poor.

We should like to add a word on the subject of abilities and the labour market in a wider sense, i.e. in relation to the contemporary economic order both within national boundaries and on the international scene. Sharpened mental abilities engender a person's responsiveness to wage structures, to total rewards or to opportunity sets. Set this human quality (acquired by the poor) within a context of severe economic duality in contemporary Asia — the result is a 'brain overflow'[4] towards centres of development or 'growth poles'. International market linkages set this flow in motion, first from rural to urban areas and then from Asia to the advanced countries of the West. This resource movement has far-reaching implications for resource utilisation as well as for incomes and income distribution, especially in relation to the new bearers of that human quality or ability. However, the characteristic response of many governments to this situation has been to curtail or control this flow while paying little attention to the causes. Moreover, the solutions chosen are regressive, i.e. anti-poor, and condone multiple deprivation as a fact of life. The sporadic attempts that have been made to change the situation are extremely modest in relation to the gravity of the problem.

Notes

1. ILO, *Matching Employment Opportunities and Expectations: A Programme of Action for Ceylon* (Geneva, ILO, 1971), p. 138.
2. M. Blaug, *Education and the Employment Problem in Developing Countries* (Geneva, ILO, 1973), p. 67.
3. These abilities are not necessarily the specific vocational skills which can be best learned on the job or by other forms of short-term training, athough even in that respect the reward structure of the labour market is a reasonably good guide.
4. This term is analytically superior to 'brain drain'; it highlights the need for improving the economic situation in the country or area of origin.

INDEX

Abilities 173, 183, 185
   distribution 9
   effects of educational expansion 9
   effects of schools 18-20
   home factors 12, 173
   learning outcomes 149-50
   learning to learn 174
   productivity 22-3
   see also scholastic achievement
Adams, D. 113
Age and education, Sri Lanka 126-8
Age and labour markets 43
Agricultural Economics Research Centre, New Delhi 113
Ahluwalia, M.S. 9n1, n4
Alexander, L. and J. Simmons 19n12
Anand, S. 25n2
Anderson, C.A. and M.J. Bowman 14n2
Anti-poverty programmes 21
Aptitude tests 183
Arachchi, U. 133
Asian Programme of Educational Innovations for Development 148, 152
Asian Regional Team for Employment Promotion 163-4
Atkinson, A.B. 77
Attitudes 183-4

Barnabas, A.P. 111-12
Barrio Schools, the Philippines 144, 148, 158
   see also survey of outcomes of elementary education (SOUTELE)
Basic education 182, 184-5
Beebout, H.S. 21n18
Blalock, H.M. 95n23
Blaug, M. 25n5, 183
Bloom, B.S. 17n4, 62n4
Book grants, Bihar 119
Boudon, R. 9n2
Brown, B.W. and D.H. Saks 19n11, 85n9

Carter, C.O. 20n17

Castes, India 113-21 *passim*, 143
   associations 111, 118, 143
   occupations 112, 113
   scheduled castes and scheduled tribes 116-21
Castillo, G.T. 144
Chaudri, D.P. 22n22
Chiswick, B. 9n3
Chiswick, C.U. 25n2
Chitnis, S. 119-20
Commissioner for Scheduled Castes and Scheduled Tribes 120n19
Committee on Non-School-Going Children, Sri Lanka 123n26
Comprehension skill in reading 57-60
   advanced countries 57
   Chile, India, Iran 58-60
Coombs, P.H. 151n18

Deprivation, multiple 12, 178-81, 185
Desai, A.R. 111, 113, 140n34
Disparities in education
   developing and advanced countries 57-60
   enrolment, Thailand 135-7
   regional disparities, Thailand 135-9; Sri Lanka 128-9; the Philippines 81-5
Distribution of education by occupation 38-43
Diyasena, W. 156n13
Dore, R. 27n6, 166, 171n24
Driver, E.D. 113
Drop-outs
   and enrolment, India 111-12, 114-16
   in Maharashtra 119
   in Sri Lanka 121-31 *passim*
   in the Philippines 144-5
   non-school-going children, Sri Lanka 123-5
   reasons for drop-out in India 111, 116-17; in Sri Lanka 125-9

Educated unemployment 33, 51-4, 145

188 Index

see also qualification inflation
Education and earnings 25, 27
  employment change 33
  income effects 54
  interaction with age 26, 43
  interaction with labour market 27, 31, 43
  linkages and interpretation 28-34
Education and labour markets 38
  distribution of education and income 45-9
  income by occupation 49-51
  job competition 52-4
  occupational structure 40
  see also educated unemployment; qualification inflation
Educational policy making 138-45, 163-9 *passim*
  distribution of school expenditures 139
  historical perspectives 141-2
  incentives, alien cultures 141
  in India 146
  manpower requirements 145
  organisation and control 142
  practical subjects 163-6
  private school initiative 143-4
  ruralisation 168-9
  unenforcability of attendance 139
  vocationalisation 161-3
  see also educated unemployment
Enrolment
  Asia 34
  Bangladesh, primary 121, 142
  India: caste 119-20; college 143-4; primary 110, 111, 115
  Sri Lanka, females 123-4
  University enrolment, Sri Lanka 131-5; ethnic composition 132; geographical disparities 134-5; income and field of study 133; sex disparities 134
Epstein, T.S. 112
Equality in education
  abilities 62
  allocation of resources 21, 178-82
  axioms 20-2
  common curriculum 14
  definitions 14
  equality of results 14
  'pure' effect of schooling 16
  reference points 15-16
  sex parity in the Philippines: in literacy 80; National College Entrance Examination Results 82; school attendance rates 81-2
Examination system 183

Fiscal policy 31
Freire, P. 18n7
Functional literacy 160, 166-8
  see also educational policies; innovations in education
Fund for Assistance to Private Education (FAPE) 85n11, 105-6

Gnanamuttu, G.A. 141n35
Grossman, M. 22n20

Hartog, J. 62n3, 185
Hoerr, O.D. 25n4
Huberman, A.M. 148n1

Illich, I.D. 18n8
Income distribution
  and occupational structure 11, 55-6
  by education in the Philippines and Sri Lanka 47-8
  by occupation in the Philippines and Sri Lanka 46-7
  distribution of education and income 45-9
  job competition and wage competition models 31-3, 52-3
  parental occupation and child achievement 10, 26, 175; *see also* scholastic achievement
  relative wages and incomes 49-51
Indian Education Commission 118, 120, 140-3, 145, 161
Innovations in education
  allocation of education resources 150
  and inequality 148-69 *passim*
  classification 151-2
  description 152-69 *passim*; affective domain 156-9; cognitive domain 152-6; manipulative skills 159-60
  distributional patterns of abilities 149
  effects of innovations 170-1
  general features 160; functionalisation 160, 166-8; practical subjects 163; ruralisation 160, 168; vocationalisation 156-7,

Index

160-1, 165-6
reference points 148
International Educational Achievement Association (IEA) 17
International Educational Achievement Association (IEA) Data Bank 71n14
International Labour Organisation 162n20, 163n22, n23, 164n25, 183n1
Islam, T. 121

Jayasuriya, J.E. 163n24
Jencks, C.S. and M.D. Brown 18n9
Job competition 174

Kim, J. and F.J. Kohout 95n22
Krathwohl, D.R. 17n5, 62n2

Labour market functioning 31, 33, 179, 184
Lallez, R. 168n32
Leonor, M.D. 22n22, 66n7, 75n21, 95n22, 148n2, 171n1
Lewin, R. 21n19
Lydall, H. 62n3, 185

Maitra, T. 114
Management of local schools, India 142-3
Mandelbaum, D.G. 111, 118
Manlapaz, R.L. 97n25
Manpower requirements approach 139, 145
Mehran, F. 97n27
Michael, R.T. 22n20, n21
Mincer, J. 9n3
Ministry of Education, Sri Lanka 128, 157n17
Ministry of Education, Thailand, 161n18

National Council of Educational Research and Training, New Delhi (NCERT) 111, 115
National Labour Institute, New Delhi 146
Nie, N. 95n22
Noonan, R. and H. Wold 19n10

Part-time education 141
Peaker, G.F. 62n2, 64n5
Potar, N. 155n11
Prantilla, B. (ed.) 100n29

Pre-vocational studies, Sri Lanka 156-8, 165-6
Primary education
  Bangladesh 121
  India 110-20 *passim*
  Sri Lanka 121-31 *passim*
  the Philippines 89-97
Project Impact 156-7
Pupil samples 63
  India, Iran, Thailand 63-4
  International Educational Achievement Association study 63
  Survey of outcomes of elementary education (SOUTELE) 90

Qualification inflation 38-43, 174, 184

Rates of return to education 25, 29
Reverse discrimination 185
Roberts, M. 142n38
Rosenthal, D.B. 143, 146
Rudolph, L.I. and S.H. 141n36
Ruralisation 168-9

Scholarships and stipends, India 119-20
Scholastic achievement 63, 71-6
  and occupation of parents 63-71
  comparative indicators 65-6
  deprivation 79
  International Educational Achievement Association results 66-71; Australia, New Zealand, Sweden 66; common features 71-6; India 67-8; Iran 68-70; Philippines 85-100 *passim*; Thailand 71; *see also* equality in education, sex parity in the Philippines; survey of outcomes of elementary education
Schultz, T.W. 22n21, 62n3, 185
Seshadri, C. 14n3
Silva de, C.R. 135n32
Simon, H.A. 95n23
Survey of outcomes of elementary education (SOUTELE) 90-5

Tamil schools, Sri Lanka 141
Taubman, P. 20n17
Theil, H. 97n17
Thorndike, R.L. 57n1, n3, 59n5, 60

Thorow, L. 9n3
Tinbergen, J. 62n3, 185
Torney, J.V. 20n14

United Nations (UN) 141n37
United Nations Economic and Social
    Commission for Asia and the Far
    East (UNESCAP) 165
United Nations Educational, Scientific and Cultural Organization
    (UNESCO) 33n7, 148, 152, 166

Vocationalisation 161-3

Wage policies 33, 53-4, 144
Walker, D.A. 20n16, 57n2, 58
Welch, F. 22n22, 62n3, 185
Wood, G. 143
Work experience programme 164